The Creation and Re-creation of Music

A New Approach to Music Fundamentals

David M. Key

Prentice Hall Englewood Cliffs New Jersey 07632

Library of Congress Cataloging-in-Publication Data
Key, David M.
    The creation and re-creation of music: a new approach to music fundamentals / David M. Key
        p. cm.
    ISBN 0–13–189622–9
    1. Music—Theory, Elementary.   2. Music appreciation.   I. Title
MT7.K4 1995   93–33536
781.2—dc20   CIP
                                                              MN

Acquisitions editor: Norwell Therien
Editorial/production supervision, page layout, and interior design: Jenny Moss
Cover design: Maureen Eide
Production coordinator: Robert Anderson
Editorial assistant: Kathy Shawhan

George Crumb's *Madrigals Book One* on page 65:
Copyright © 1971 by C. F. Peters Corporation. Used by permission.

John Cage's Concert for Piano and Orchestra on page 66:
Copyright © 1960 by Henmar Press Inc. Used by permission of C. F. Peters Corporation.

 © 1995 by Prentice-Hall, Inc.
A Paramount Communications Company
Englewood Cliffs, New Jersey   07632

Printed in the United States of America
10   9   8   7   6   5   4   3   2   1

ISBN 0-13-189622-9

Prentice-Hall International (UK) Limited, *London*
Prentice-Hall of Australia Pty. Limited, *Sydney*
Prentice-Hall Canada Inc., *Toronto*
Prentice-Hall Hispanoamericana, S.A., *Mexico*
Prentice-Hall of India Private Limited, *New Delhi*
Prentice-Hall of Japan, Inc., *Tokyo*
Simon & Schuster Asia Pte. Ltd., *Singapore*
Editora Prentice-Hall do Brasil, Ltda., *Rio de Janeiro*

For Cathy

Contents

Cassette Tape Selections

Preface

INTRODUCTION

The Creation and Re-creation of Music: A New Approach to Music Fundamentals was written for use by the student with little or no background in music. Within the present structure of music education, the text will fill the needs of the student in a one-semester basic musicianship course, though the material will take student and teacher outside the scope of a "typical" basic musicianship class. Intended as an introduction to the basic materials of music, *The Creation and Re-creation of Music* involves the student in the process of music making in three important ways:

1. Through the development of critical listening skills
2. Through individual and group creative assignments
3. Through guided journal writings

Basic materials are introduced in the body of the text, and their application to the process of music creation is explored through the exercises listed above. A careful use of the text and accompanying tape will lead to

A better understanding of music composition and performance
An ability to create original music that is organized and artistic
A greater sensitivity to the workings of music in our society

Music notation is introduced through modeling exercises, which lead in a very natural way to the reading and writing of notated music. All areas of the text involve the student in the *creation* of music, and treat the written aspect as the *re-creation* of music.

TEXT FORMAT

Most chapters of *The Creation and Re-creation of Music* follow a similar pattern:

Chapter material is introduced and discussed.

The Creative Process, or a similar section, provides a summary through a discussion of the application of chapter material to the creative process.

Listening Assignments ask the student to apply what has been learned in the chapter to the process of critical listening.

A Creative Assignment with specific guidelines directs the student in the development of an original musical creation that utilizes chapter material.

Echo Pattern Assignments (Chapters 1–4) develop a basic rhythmic and melodic vocabulary through modeling techniques.

Performance Assignments (found in later chapters) provide practice in the notational aspects of music.

Journal Entry Suggestions provide possible topics for personal journal entries dealing with music.

Accompanying Tape

The cassette tape that accompanies the text is an integral part of the learning process. Frequent Listening Examples, marked with a cassette icon in the text, accompany many chapters (especially in Parts 1 and 2). These excerpts, often short in length, provide aural examples of the application of chapter material. The tape also has Listening Assignments and Echo Pattern Assignments.

The examples on the tape are varied. Some are classical pieces that might be known; others are twentieth-century works that are less familiar. Selections include Japanese shakuhachi flute music, whale songs, pop and rock music, pieces from American musicals, and traditional songs of a few European countries. Although it is not the intent of the text or of the author to provide a comprehensive source of listening examples, these examples will show the varied ways in which materials can be used and will expose the student to some of the wealth of the world's music.

The accompanying tape is an important part of the text and should not be considered an optional component of the package. The tape introduces the student to the language of music and provides the first step in the development of a listening and performing vocabulary. This vocabulary, in turn, serves as a base for subsequent discussions of music's more theoretical aspects. The tape initiates much of the early learning of melodic and rhythmic notation.

Creative Assignments

An important part of the text involves the personal exploration of how music works, using regular individual and group Creative Assignments. Early Creative Assignments presuppose a limited music background with no experience in the reading of music. The assignments progressively demand more sophistication of the student in combining the elements of music in creative ways, and in notating assignments more specifically. Most Creative Assignments ask the student to save the assignment on tape; a few ask the student to be prepared to perform in class or to participate in a class group assignment. Later assignments ask students to apply their newly-learned notation skills to saving assignments. The Creative Assignments, an important part of this text, are meant to be an exploratory *process* leading to the synthesis of information and ideas.

The Music Journal

Throughout the text, students are encouraged to become *involved* in the materials of music. Guided Listening Exercises and Creative Assignments ask the student to take an active role in the process of understanding music. Experiencing music through critical listening and through personal composition will foster a deeper understanding of and appreciation for the "creation and re-creation" of music. The process of writing about music and about the ways in which it touches our lives in a very personal sense is another important part of learning about music.

Each student is asked to keep a personal Music Journal and to write in the journal as frequently as possible (daily entries are encouraged). Although the text includes suggestions for journal entries, these are *suggestions* only. The content of the journal is left up to the student. One student may experiment with turning off the TV's sound while watching a cartoon, commenting on the effect this has on the impact of the program. Another might notice a recently studied music concept at work in the "real world."

The Music Journal is a place for recognizing music at work outside the classroom. It is a place for quiet thinking or for exuberant remarks about a recently attended concert. The journal is reserved for personal observations and ideas, and is not the place to be concerned about grammar and spelling. Even though space is provided in the text for journal entries, each student should keep a separate journal that can be periodically evaluated in a nonjudgmental way.

Some examples of different types of journal entries are the following:

I was watching television the other night, flipping through the channels and noticing how the commercials were so beefed up by the music that was playing in the background. So I wondered what this one commercial would sound like without music and it was amazing how dead it was when I turned the volume down. Everything besides talk shows and some others has music in it and nothing would seem right if it didn't.

Reviewing for my test, I'm listening to the tape . . . and when I heard "And God Created Great Whales" by Hovhaness, I was listening to it in a different perspective. I heard a lot of brass, very ceremonial sounding, and I thought about how trumpets have been named to be royal instruments, and that fit along with "God and the Great Whales." So then I was thinking about the possibility that the composer chose the brass instruments for that purpose. To me, it makes sense that these instruments (trumpet, etc.) would be used to perform greatness and even create it.

Summary

The variety of approaches used by the text are intended to serve as a catalyst for learning. The material absorbed from these pages is just one part of the learning process. In order for the new student of music to learn about this wonderful, complex subject matter, it is important for the student to *explore* it, and to become involved with the "stuff" of music as it is found in his or her own life. If, after spending time with this material, the student finds that music is no longer in the background of life, but has become a conscious part of day-to-day activities, *The Creation and Re-creation of Music* will have attained one of its goals. If, in addition, the student *remains* a student of music, even after the completion of the coursework, the main goal of the text will have been realized.

ACKNOWLEDGMENTS

I am grateful to Bud Therien, publisher at Prentice Hall, for his belief in me and in this project; I also appreciate the time, energy, and professional commitment of the reviewers—Jonathan Berger, Yale University; Robert L. Borg, University of Minnesota; James C. Burge, Hillsborough Community College; Karl E. Gambert, Edinboro University of Pennsylvania; James Greeson, University of Arkansas; Patricia Hackett, San Francisco State University; Tom Risher, University of North Alabama; and Deborah Teplow, Foothill College—and editors of this text. Special thanks to Jenny Moss for her untiring work as production editor and to Jim Wayne for his integrity and dogged determination in putting together the tape. I would like to thank Dennis Pratt for his early recognition and quiet development of my talent, and Dick Grunow, who inspired me to move in new directions in music education and whose rhythm and melodic modeling techniques I've used throughout this text. Thanks to Gene Pollart, who has consistently believed in me, even when I've doubted myself. I am thankful for my students—they have been and continue to be my real teachers. My thanks to family and friends, especially Andy Lustig, whose friendship and encouragement during the years have helped me immensely. This book is gratefully dedicated to Cathy Jacques, whose loving support has nurtured my own creative energies. Her ability to find the childlike quality in all of life continues to inspire me to express myself in creative ways.

David M. Key

PART ONE

♪♪♪♪♪♪

The Basic Materials of Music

Music is everywhere. We hear it in the elevator and at the store. We listen to it at home and at work; while we study and while we clean the house. Because music serves so many functions in our lives, we can easily take it for granted. Listening passively to music can allow this powerful art form to fade into the background of our lives; to lose its individuality, its beauty, its expressive capabilities. To fully understand and appreciate music, we must separate it from its many roles. We must begin to listen to music on its own terms.

When we listen to music, we often bring to the experience some extramusical baggage. A new piece might sound menacing to us because it reminds us of the background music for a suspense movie. This process of association can be very subtle, and the resulting feeling very strong. If we link an event, person, or feeling with a specific piece of music or a particular sound, that link will be made each time we hear the piece. In some cases, this is appropriate. Sometimes, though, strong associations can prejudice our listening experience. We can overcome this prejudice by developing good listening habits.

We can listen to a selection more than once, finding new levels of meaning each time. We can learn more about the piece, how it was composed or performed, how its ideas and sounds are organized. We can unearth background information that is relevant to the piece. These are just a few ways of bringing our emotional and intellectual experiences to the listening process. If we continue to develop our listening skills, we will have a more complete understanding of music and a more enjoyable listening experience.

The first example on the accompanying cassette tape is the sound of a humpback whale "singing." Although no one is entirely sure how or why whales sing, many believe it to be a form of communication for these mammals. Before noisy powerboats were introduced to the environment, whales were capable of hearing each others' songs even when a thousand miles apart. This distance has been decreased dramatically with the noise pollution of our oceans, but whales still sing to each other.

Though some would not credit whales with the ability to actually compose music, their songs do exhibit an artistic organization and development of material. Their compositions show a balance of repetition and variety. While other animals (like birds) have ornate patterns of song, whales seem to actually compose new works—each year humpback whales are heard singing and exchanging a new song. Whale songs may seem eerie at first, but continued exposure to this natural music will help you become more comfortable with this new form.

 Humpback Whale Song

It seems that humans have long been fascinated with natural sounds. As we will see later, some of the earliest musical instruments evolved from found objects such as hollow logs and rams' horns. Even with the present-day availability of sophisticated electronic instruments, some composers and performers choose to use natural and found sounds in their works. The next two selections on the listening tape demonstrate this, weaving whale songs into original compositions.

Paul Winter is fond of using wolf howls, birdcalls, and whale songs in his music. In "Ocean Dream," the whale song serves as a basic melodic idea that Winter sets to appropriate lyrics.

 Winter, "Ocean Dream"

Alan Hovhaness uses whales as instruments in a composition for orchestra. In this work, whale songs serve as source material not only for the music but for an extramusical pictorial representation of the world before human existence, of vast undersea mountains and a wide ocean sky.

Hovhaness, "And God Created Great Whales"

THE BASIC ELEMENTS OF MUSIC

Developing sensitive listening skills can help us better understand music. We can also improve our understanding by taking a closer look at the process of music making, and by creating music of our own. Recognizing the basic elements of music and discovering ways in which these elements can be organized is the first step in this process.

According to one definition, music is the presentation of organized sounds in time. As such, music is usually considered a human form of expression; one reason why some would not accept whale songs as music. It is true that music often seems to reflect the life patterns of humans. People develop relationships and make choices in life, tension develops and is resolved, there are high points and low. Music has similar patterns in its structure. The composer develops relationships between sounds and musical ideas and makes decisions about which musical ideas are more important; musical tension is developed, reaches a high point, and then is resolved. All of these structural concepts have their purpose in music, but it is the general idea of tension and relaxation that serves as an important core in the music composition process.

The general contour of tension and relaxation will be seen clearly in later chapters, when we discuss melody, rhythm, and musical form. This pattern of tension and relaxation can also be seen in the extremes of music's basic elements of pitch, intensity, duration, and timbre.

Pitch

Pitch is the element of music that deals with high and low sounds. Though not all sounds have pitch, the majority of sources used to create music produce pitched sounds. Sound is created when a sound source sets the air vibrating. A sound source such as a flute will produce even, or consistent, vibrations. The number of vibrations is given in cycles per second (cps), with higher pitches having a greater frequency and a higher number of cps. Lower pitches will have a smaller number of cps. These even vibrations produce a sound with a definite pitch—we can recognize a specific high or low sound.

Ex. 1.1

When vibrations are uneven, sounds of indefinite pitch are heard—we cannot pick out a specific high or low sound (although the sound may have a general highness or lowness to it). Smacking a hand against a table-top produces a sound with an indefinite pitch. The simplified waveform of a sound with indefinite pitch might look like this:

Ex. 1.2

Some musical instruments (like cymbals) produce sounds of indefinite pitch. Outside the musical world, these sounds would be considered "noise." Through careful organization and presentation, however, these sounds can be used in the making of music.

Most sound sources used in music have very complex waveforms, more complex than the simplified versions used for our examples. Like human fingerprints, each instrument's waveform is unique. The shape of an instrument's waveform is one distinctive characteristic that helps deter-mine its individual sound.

Intensity

The amplitude, or size, of the sound wave determines the loudness, or intensity, of a sound.

Ex. 1.3

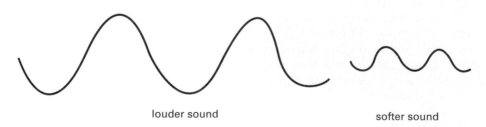

louder sound   softer sound

When instruments are played together, their combined intensity levels may be changed in one or more of three ways:

Terraced: adding instruments to produce a louder sound; taking instruments away to produce a softer sound. This is a common change in popular styles (as well as in other styles).

Sudden: all instruments immediately change together from one level of intensity to another.

Gradual: instruments change intensity levels together a little at a time.

Typically, a piece of music demonstrates more than one type of intensity change, often in various combinations.

Duration

The length of time a sound is heard is called the *duration* of the sound. Duration has the following components:

Attack: the initiation of the sound. An attack may be sharp, with a sudden, pronounced beginning, or smooth, with a gradual beginning to the sound. Often the attack is a degree of these two extremes.

Sustain: the part of the sound from the peak, or leveling-off of the attack, to the beginning of the decay.

Decay: the beginning of the loss of amplitude (intensity) of the sound. The amount of time the sound takes to completely die away can vary—the decay may be sudden, gradual, or somewhere between.

Attack, sustain, and decay combine to form an instrument's unique *envelope* of sound. An acoustic guitar played with a pick will have a fairly sharp attack, a short sustain, and a quick decay. Compared with the acoustic guitar, an acoustic piano has a longer sustain and a more gradual decay, while its sharp attack will be similar to the guitar's.

Timbre

Timbre is the term for tone color in music. The particular sound that an instrument makes and the sound produced by different combinations of instruments give us this basic element of music. A flute, playing a specific pitch for a certain length of time, at a particular level of intensity, sounds different from a saxophone playing the same pitch at the same level of intensity for the same length of time. Likewise, the combination of flute and saxophone sounds different from a combination of oboe and bassoon. Timbre can be an important element in the creative process of music; we explore this element in greater detail in Chapter 3.

THE CREATIVE PROCESS

The creation of music involves the organization and artistic presentation of pitch, intensity, duration, and timbre. Sounds with definite pitch are most often used, though sounds with indefinite pitch can be used in a musical way as well. Choices concerning intensity levels and types of intensity changes are made during the composition process. Notes of varying pitch and duration are combined to create and resolve tension, and combinations of different types of sound sources provide various timbres. In its organization, music has definite sections, with points of rest, called *cadence points,* that divide the work into recognizable units. Cadence points occur at points of relaxation in music, signaling either a temporary resting point or the end of a section or a complete work. The final resolution of tension usually happens after a high point, the *climax,* is reached. After the climax, the work may resolve either suddenly or gradually, with a *final cadence.*

When we listen to a piece of music, we should concentrate on hearing and identifying the choices made by the composer concerning the organization of the music's basic elements. When we create our own music, we should organize sounds and ideas and create a balance between the extremes of high and low, long and short, loud and soft, and tension and relaxation. This will help us produce our own artistic piece of music.

LISTENING ASSIGNMENT

(examples found on accompanying tape)

A. What types of intensity changes can be heard in each example?

   1.

   2.

   3.

B. For each example, describe the *envelope* of sound, comprising the *attack* (sharp or smooth), *sustain* (long or short), and *decay* (sudden or gradual):

   1. attack

   sustain

   decay

   2. attack

   sustain

   decay

3. attack

sustain

decay

C. For each example, comment on the choices the composer or arranger made concerning pitch, intensity, and duration. Are sounds generally high or low, loud or soft? What types of intensity changes does the composer use?

1.

2.

CREATIVE ASSIGNMENT

This exercise begins with some critical listening and thinking on your part. Choose one of the following scenes or situations:

breaking glass
a storm
city sounds

Listen carefully to or think specifically about pitch, intensity, duration, and timbre as they apply to your chosen scene. Are the sounds high in pitch, low in pitch, or varying? Are the sounds mostly definite or indefinite in pitch? Is there a steady level of intensity, or does it change? If intensity changes, does it do so in a terraced manner, or suddenly or gradually? Are the sounds short in duration, or long? How can you describe the envelope of sounds used? How can the timbre or timbres used be described?

Once you have spent some time analyzing the treatment of the basic elements of music in your scene, use your imagination to recreate the scene yourself. Use found objects such as pots and pans, stones, and other common items, or traditional instruments like a piano used in nontraditional ways. Create the pitch, intensity, duration, and timbre changes that will give a fair representation of the scene you have chosen. Experiment with various ideas and combinations. When you are satisfied with the result, tape your effort on your Creative Assignment tape.

ECHO PATTERN ASSIGNMENT

(examples found on accompanying tape)

Listen to each of the rhythm echo patterns. Perform Chapter 1 echo patterns 1 through 4, keeping a steady beat and repeating each using the rhythm syllables. When you have mastered these patterns, use the appropriate syllables to perform examples 5 through 8. Melodic patterns then follow—use appropriate melodic syllables, as heard on the tape, for these examples.

JOURNAL ENTRY SUGGESTIONS

What is music?

Try to spend some time noticing sounds that occur in nature. Keep a log of those sounds that you consider to be musical. Comment on the characteristics that make you feel that way about those sounds.

How do you distinguish between "sound" and "noise"?

♪♪♪♪♪♪

Responding to Music

A composer or performer who creates music chooses combinations and treatments of basic elements to present a coherent musical statement. If he or she is successful in combining ideas, moving to a climax, and resolving tension in an artistic way, the work will stand the chance of being understood by at least some listeners. But the connection from composer to performer to listener is a tenuous one. Each of us, as a link in the chain, must accept the responsibilities of the role we play.

As listeners, we interpret the music we hear. Even if our interpretation is not in line with the composer's original intent, it will be valid if we accept the responsibility to understand the composer's intent as best we can. Music is an art form; no matter how much we try to codify and compartmentalize the creative process of music making, there is always room for personal interpretation. This places on the listener the responsibility to bring as much as possible to the listening experience. We must recognize and understand the ways in which we respond to music.

THE PHYSICAL–EMOTIONAL LEVEL OF RESPONSE

Of all of music's components, sound is its most important. Only with music do we find an art form that relies almost entirely on the organization of sound to produce its results. With its celebration of the very sounds of words, poetry comes close but at some point must deal with more than the physical sensation of sound. The richness of the sense and symbol of words is always present and becomes an important part of most poetry. In contrast, the sense of music comes from the organization and presentation of sound waves. As a result our first response to music is often a physical one.

We respond to extremes in life. This is often true in our response to music. Hearing a singer reach a stratospheric pitch or an ensemble perform at a high level of intensity gives us a feeling of excitement. At the other extreme, hearing music that continues for a period of time at a low level of intensity produces the tension of straining to hear a whispered secret. Lively rhythms and a strong beat can lead the listener to tap his or her foot or dance to the physical sensation of music. "It had a good beat and was easy to dance to" or "That song makes me feel like crying"—our most primal responses are *physical* or *emotional*.

The Greeks believed that different combinations of pitches produce different emotional responses in the listener. One melody, so they thought, would cause sadness; a different one would lead the listener to feel happy or content. The European Baroque musician some time later expanded on this idea with the *doctrine of affections*. This theory suggested that the body's main "humors" (spiritual vapors and fluids) were physically excited by certain types of music. The "sad" humor would respond to one type of melody, while "peaceful and content" humors would be physically stirred by a different melody. Composers during this time followed this idea so closely that it became difficult to tell if listeners were responding in certain ways to certain sounds or if they were becoming conditioned to associate feelings and reactions with specific melodic combinations.

THE ASSOCIATIVE LEVEL OF RESPONSE

Although sound is music's primary concern, there is more to the art form. The most basic response to music is on the physical–emotional level, but we often respond on the *associative* level, as well. Many times a piece of music has lyrics or has a story line or other nonmusical idea connected with it. Such music is called *program music*. Unlike *absolute music*, which has no story line or text connected with it, an important component of program music is the extramusical element.

Even when a piece of music does not have associative elements, we as listeners might find ourselves responding in an associative way, making a connection between the music and a memory or extramusical idea of our own. A certain song that was playing on the radio the moment your girlfriend or boyfriend broke up with you now makes you feel sad each time you hear it. You will be brought back to that moment each time you hear the song; in your mind the song has become associated with the event.

Any time a piece of music reminds us of something, we are responding on the associative level. Even when we hear a piece of music for the first time, we tend to picture a scene or occurrence to match the music. Sounds that are new to us (like humpback whale songs) are especially prone to this phenomenon. We generalize about the sound of "scary" or "sad" when we are confronted by a new piece. Perhaps the Greeks were right after all—different melodic combinations evoke different responses.

Associative responses can be very compelling and do not always occur on the conscious level. The motion-picture industry, among others, takes advantage of our subconscious associative responses. In the movie *Jaws,* for example, a low-pitched, "sneaky" sound lets the viewer know that the great white shark is nearby. Sustained horn calls that follow signal the shark's swift approach. We know that some helpless swimmer will soon become the predator's victim.

While many motion pictures have music composed specifically for them, others rely on previously composed music, and on the associative responses that music evokes. Samuel Barber's "Adagio for Strings" was brought to the movie *Platoon* already rich in associations. This work, with its sustained string sounds that gradually build in intensity and pitch to a high climax, is very moving, even for the first-time listener. The music has such emotional strength (the Greeks again!) that it has come to be heard as an expression of extreme sorrow; the "Adagio" has been used at many funeral services. *Platoon* counts on these emotional and associative responses, but the filmmakers were not content to match the music with complementary scenes in the movie. A feeling of unease and a sense of irony are created when scenes of intensity and violence are accompanied by Barber's serene, peaceful "Adagio for Strings."

Sometimes associative connections in the film industry are more individual in nature. *Star Trek II: The Wrath of Khan* provides an example of this. At the end of the movie, a funeral service is held aboard the *Enterprise* for Spock, who has sacrificed himself to save the ship and its crew. As the coffin begins to move slowly toward an eject hatch, Scotty (Lieutenant Commander Scott) plays "Amazing Grace" on the highland bagpipe. Although Scotty's Scottish heritage is reason enough for this tribute, there is another story behind the scene. At the time of the production of *Star Trek II,* one of the executive producers had attended a funeral service in Great Britain for someone in the British military. As custom dictated, "Amazing Grace" was played on the pipes during the service. The producer was so moved by this experience that he fought for the inclusion of the bagpipe in the movie, even though a number of people disagreed with his decision. This is an example of a personal associative connection being so strong that an individual felt the need to share the experience with the viewers of a movie.

Often there is a close connection between the story line and the music that helps portray the story. Sergei Prokofiev, a Russian composer, wrote music to accompany the 1933 film *Lieutenant Kije.* The film's story is based on a Russian czar's mistake while reading a roster of army personnel. The czar adds a Lieutenant Kije to the list. Rather than correct their leader, the czar's courtiers follow up on the mistake and create a complete life for the fictitious lieutenant. Of course, Kije is the perfect man as well as the perfect Russian military hero. The film and the music satirize government bureaucracy at its worst.

Prokofiev used material from the film's score to create a work for orchestra, *Lieutenant Kije Suite*. The work portrays some of the major events in Kije's life, with sections entitled "The Birth of Kije," "Romance," "The Wedding of Kije," "Troika" (a Russian sleigh ride), and "Burial of Kije."

Some fifty years later, Sting made an associative connection one step removed from the one Prokofiev made. One of the founders of the popular group "The Police," Sting is a solo pop artist who enjoys making references in his music to literary themes and to other forms and styles of music. Sting uses Prokofiev's "Romance" theme from the *Lieutenant Kije Suite* in his own composition "Russians." This piece deals with the delicate situation that existed between the United States and Russia during the time of Nikita Khrushchev and that continued when Ronald Reagan was the U.S. president. Sting contended that though these men of power may have been able to comprehend an exchange of nuclear weapons, the average Russian, who "loves his children, too," did not want to see such a military action take place. Sting used the lyrical "Romance" theme to make a positive emotional connection between our culture and that of Russia. In using a portion of the *Lieutenant Kije Suite,* he also satirized the position of the leaders of both countries, reminding us of the situation that led to the original story of Lieutenant Kije.

Other pop composers and performers have incorporated classical themes into their work. Eric Carmen, a pop artist of the 1970s, used a Rachmaninoff theme for "All By Myself." Paul Simon worked for years with Art Garfunkel. Shortly after striking out on his own he wrote "American Tune," which is a direct quote of a chorale by Johann Sebastian Bach. Both of these examples use the quoted material for its own sake; we can still respond on the physical–emotional level. In his use of Prokofiev's music, Sting allows us to respond in an emotional way but also asks us to respond on the associative level. Even more, to provide the intended impact he counts on the listener's knowledge of Prokofiev's music. Sting asks for more than an emotional response and goes beyond making a simple associative connection. He asks for an *intellectual* response as well, requiring that the listener of "Russians" know something of Prokofiev's work.

THE INTELLECTUAL LEVEL OF RESPONSE

You have already begun to respond to music in an intellectual way. Listening for ways in which basic elements are used in a piece, identifying types of intensity changes, and commenting on the structure and organization of music are all intellectual responses. As you continue to develop a listening and creative vocabulary, you will be able to respond more fully to music that you hear, even for the first time. You will be aware of your emotional and physical reactions and will recognize associative connections. By including intellectual responses, you will begin to have a more complete, holistic listening experience.

Some knowledge of the composer and performer can enhance the listening event. Knowing the story line of *Lieutenant Kije Suite* can give you a greater understanding of the meaning behind Sting's "Russians." Learning the background of the lyrics in a particular song can provide you with a greater depth of interpretation of the piece. There are many ways that a more intellectual approach can enrich the process of listening to music. We as listeners must not be afraid to use any and all means available to provide us with a complete listening experience.

THE CREATIVE PROCESS

When we combine musical ideas of our own, we might find ourselves creating music in response to the same categories we use when we are listening: physical–emotional, associative, and intellectual.

In creating music, we might use a particular combination of sounds simply because we are taken with the properties of the sounds themselves; the sensation of the sounds is appealing, so we make our choices accordingly. Decisions we make about pitch, intensity, and duration might also be determined by what we hear as being "right." We might discover a certain pulse or rhythmic idea through the physical sensation of tapping on a tabletop. We might find ourselves imitating a pattern heard in our environment. Any number of physical–emotional processes could guide us in our choices.

Many works of music are programmatic in nature. The Creative Assignment in Chapter 1 asked you to create a piece of program music, choosing a particular scene to represent musically. For that assignment, you were asked to create a piece that would evoke an associative response in the listener. What is interesting about the process, though, is the fact that you also needed to involve the *intellectual* aspects of the creative process. If you chose to portray a storm, you needed to analyze the ways in which the properties of pitch, intensity, and duration were utilized. You needed to make decisions about sound sources and the treatment of sounds based on an analysis of the storm creation process. To evoke an associative response in the listener, you needed to incorporate all three levels (physical–emotional, associative, and intellectual) into the creative process.

A more "pure" form of associative creation is involved when lyrics are present. When composing music for use with lyrics, we need to be aware of a number of elements:

general mood: what is the basic message of the text? Is it an upbeat, happy one, or something more serious or introspective? Setting a limerick to music demands of us a quicker, lighter melody; a more somber text requires music to match. Of course, we can choose to mismatch music and text for a particular effect, but we should be aware that we are doing so and never find ourselves in a position of inadvertently setting a text to the wrong style of music.

physical use of words: which vowel or consonant sounds seem bright? Which ones have a dark sound? Do certain words or groupings of words seem to require a quicker series of pitches or a greater emphasis? Are there words that need pitches held for a greater length of time?

tension: how is tension created in the lyrics? Where is the climax? What kind of resolution to tension is found in the lyrics—sudden or gradual; high or low?

Though we may not wish to mimic the lyrics with our music, or even complement the lyrics at all times, we need to recognize the areas described above so we can make informed decisions about the organization of the elements of music in a song. Word grouping in a text will affect our choices of duration; the sense of the lyrics may be influenced by our decisions concerning intensity and timbre. We can underscore (or undermine!) the climax and the resolution of tension found in the text. At all times, we need to be aware of the message of the lyrics and understand how our music relates to the text.

Leonard Bernstein, composer, and Stephen Sondheim, lyricist, collaborated on the song "Maria" from the Broadway musical *West Side Story.* Even though music and text were created by two different people, this selection shows a wonderful blend of the two elements, with a poetic treatment of both words and sounds. The word *Maria* becomes the focus of the piece, and of this lover's reverie.

"Maria" begins quietly, with Tony singing in a dreamlike way about his love. He talks about the fact that even the name "Maria" is the most beautiful sound he has ever heard. Bernstein's choice of instrumental timbre complements the mood. String instruments provide a warm accompaniment, with Tony's vocal solo portraying a solitary moment, a man in love. A rhythmic Latin feel reminds us of Maria's heritage, while the repetition of *Maria* signifies Tony's preoccupation with the word and the woman. Each melodic repetition of these three syllables provides a small section, a short cadence. Other words are grouped together, providing rhythmic direction and moving toward cadence points. A wide range of pitches is used, and different types of intensity changes can be heard. The key word, *Maria,* is used as soloist and orchestra move to a climax, both in pitch and intensity. The tension of the climax is resolved, and the piece ends as it began, with a man's quiet thoughts of love.

LISTENING ASSIGNMENT

A. As you listen to George Winston's arrangement of "The Holly and the Ivy," write your responses to the music. Identify the types of responses you have made as physical–emotional, associative, or intellectual.

B. Review the humpback whale song of Chapter 1 and give an intellectual response.

C. Listen to your Chapter 1 Creative Assignment "soundscene," or to that of a classmate. Identify the types of responses you have to the music. On the intellectual level, listen for the choices made concerning attack, sustain, and decay. Why were these choices made? Does one choice seem to work better than another?

D. You will hear excerpts from the first movement of Claude Debussy's String
Quartet and a portion of George Crumb's *Black Angels: Thirteen Images from
the Dark Land.* After hearing both, comment as instructed.
1. Give a physical–emotional response.

2. On the intellectual level, describe how the basic elements of pitch,
intensity, and duration are treated differently by each composer.

3. How are the pieces similar?

CREATIVE ASSIGNMENT

In preparation for this assignment, choose one of the following
poems:

Interval

Joseph Auslander

Water pulls nervously whispering satin across
     cool roots, cold stones;
     And a bird balances his soul on a song flash, a
          desperate outcry:
These are the minor chords, the monotones;
     This the undefeated gesture against an armored sky.

The moment is metal; the sun crawling over it is a fly
    Head down on a bronze ceiling; the hot stillness
        drones:
And you go sliding through green sea shafts and I
    Am an old mountain warming his tired bones.

Source: From *Sunrise Trumpets* by Joseph Auslander. Copyright © 1924 by Harper
    & Row Publishers, Inc. Copyright renewed 1952 by Joseph Auslander.
    Reprinted by permission of HarperCollins Publishers.

Nocturne
Robert Hillyer

If the deep wood is haunted, it is I
Who am the ghost; not the tall trees
Nor the white moonlight slanting down like rain,
Filling the hollows with bright pools of silver.

A long train whistle serpentines around the hill
Now shrill, now far away.
Tell me, from what dark smoky terminal
What train sets out for yesterday?

Or, since our spirits take off and resume
Their flesh as travellers their cloaks, O tell me where,
In what age and what country you will come,
That I may meet you there.

Source: From *Collected Poems* by Robert Hillyer. Copyright 1933 and renewed 1961
    by Robert Hillyer. Copyright © 1961 by Robert Hillyer. Reprinted by per-
    mission of Alfred A. Knopf, Inc.

The Two-Headed Calf
Laura Gilpin

Tomorrow when the farm boys find this
freak of nature, they will wrap his body
in newspaper and carry him to the museum.

But tonight he is alive and in the north
field with his mother. It is a perfect
summer evening: the moon rising over
the orchard, the wind in the grass. And
as he stares into the sky, there are
twice as many stars as usual.

Source: *The Hocus Pocus of the Universe* by Laura Gilpin. Copyright © 1977 by Laura
    Gilpin. Used by permission of Doubleday, a division of Bantam Doubleday
    Dell Publishing Group, Inc.

Analyze your chosen poem, following the basic points discussed on page 15. Write down your observations in these areas and in any other areas that might influence your use of pitch, intensity, duration, and timbre in an original creative exercise. Decide on the general mood and basic message of the poem, where the climax should be, and how tension might be developed. If you set the poem to music for unaccompanied voice, identify key words and possible cadence points, and do a further analysis for possible word groupings and use of rhythmic motion. Be prepared to share your observations with the class. Once you are more familiar with the poem, choose one of the following assignments:

1. Create a sound scene that gives an impression or representation of one of the poems. Your soundscene should use traditional instruments or found objects, with or without narration of the poem itself.

2. Use the text of one of the poems, setting it for unaccompanied solo voice. Try to use the poem as it is constructed, though you may repeat short sections, words, or lines, if needed.

If you feel comfortable working with traditional or nontraditional instruments, recreating the general mood and specific development of tension and relaxation in a poem, choose option 1. If you are more comfortable using your voice, setting the poem to your own created melody, try option 2. If you choose this option, be sure to use your voice in a melodic way; don't give a recitation of the poem (even a "rap recitation"). Work with the elements of music.

Either option will be challenging. The poems were chosen because of their powerful images, message, or language and are not easily modified as lyrics. What is most important is that you experiment with various sound combinations, working with changes in pitch, intensity, duration, and timbre to portray the important moments in the poem. Try to become comfortable with making a connection between text and music, even if you don't end up with a pop song.

Though creating music for solo voice is unusual in our culture and in our time, the practice of singing without accompaniment has a longstanding history. In our society, the constant backwash of sound and noise that we have become accustomed to makes the prospect of singing alone rather frightening. The sound of one voice can be a powerful way to present music and text, however. Robbie O'Connell demonstrates this with the first verse of his song "Two Nations." O'Connell, an Irish folk musician, brings the Celtic tradition of unaccompanied singing to his song.

  O'Connell, "Two Nations"

O'Connell uses a variety of pitches and demonstrates carefully planned cadence points. He uses pitch changes and intensity changes to reach a climax, after which he brings his melody to a close. Though none of the poems used for this assignment was intended as lyrics the way the text of "Two Nations" was, you should be able to find within each poem the lyricism needed to set the words to music.

ECHO PATTERN ASSIGNMENT

Use the accompanying tape to master the echo patterns for Chapter 2.

JOURNAL ENTRY SUGGESTIONS

What roles does music play in your life? Do you use music to get "pumped up"; do you dance to it? Do you listen to music while you work? Do you listen for enjoyment? Comment on the different ways music is a part of your life.

How have your own musical tastes changed during the years? What has influenced your musical tastes the most?

Turn off the sound on your television set during commercials. What do you notice when the music is absent? Now turn the sound back on. What styles of music seem to be used the most during commercials? Do different types of products use different styles of music? What associative connections do you think the manufacturers of products are trying to make, and how do they accomplish this?

♪♪♪♪♪♪

CHAPTER 3

Timbre

Each instrument has its own sound. Different instruments can be combined in a number of ways to provide a variety of tone colors, or *timbres*. One of the Listening Assignments in Chapter 2 asked you to compare a portion of a Debussy string quartet with one written by George Crumb. This grouping of instruments (two violins, viola, and cello) has been used for over two hundred years, but the possibilities for creating new tone colors with this combination are still being explored.

Composers and arrangers choose to write for different instruments for a variety of reasons. From previous experience, a composer may know what sound a certain combination will have; he or she may wish to use this well-known sonority to explore other elements of music in relative safety or comfort. A composer may be intrigued with the possibilities of a new or seldom-used ensemble and may wish to experiment with its tonal palette. Or the composer may hear a certain sound in his or her mind's ear and strive to realize that sound with a combination of instruments.

In addition to these strictly musical reasons for choosing an ensemble of instruments, some nonmusical reasons may influence a composer's choice. If he or she is presenting a piece of program music or is in some other way concerned with nurturing an associative response, certain instruments or combinations may best serve that purpose. Just as particular sounds and melodic patterns have come to be associated with certain feelings, some instruments bring with them specific associative connections. The trumpet, traditionally used to announce kings and their court, has a strong association with royalty. In the *Messiah,* George Frideric Handel uses this instrument only twice, once for the bass solo "The Trumpet Shall Sound" and again in the well-known "Hallelujah" chorus. This chorus, with its many references to Jesus as "King of Kings" and "Lord of Lords," uses the trumpet's association with royalty to full effect.

As a regal instrument, the trumpet was also used in battle, coupled with timpani (kettledrums). This historical pairing survived when these instruments were introduced into the orchestra. For some time, composers wrote for the two only in combination.

The trombone is another instrument with historical associations. Historically, it has been one of the few instruments allowed in the Christian church and has developed spiritual associative responses. In 1607, in his opera *Orfeo,* Claudio Monteverdi took advantage of this spiritual heritage, using the trombone to portray Hades. More than one hundred years later, when listeners heard the trombone in a section of his *Requiem* (mass for the dead) the associative response linking the trombone to Hades and to religion would have been understood.

Some instruments, being younger than the trumpet or trombone, have less of a heritage. The saxophone has struggled since its invention in the 1860s for acceptance in the classical world. This instrument's association with jazz and rock has limited its acceptance in the world of "serious" music, and though well-known composers have written some fine music for it, the saxophone has yet to be completely accepted as an orchestral instrument.

INSTRUMENT CATEGORIES

As we saw in Chapter 1, humans have long been fascinated with the sounds of nature. Natural sound sources have served as inspiration for imitation or inclusion in original compositions. It is likely (though we can't know for sure) that natural (found) objects were the first materials used by humans to create musical sounds. A fallen tree decaying to the point where it resonated when struck with a stick; two stones clattering together; the sound of human and animal voices—these were probably our earliest musical instruments. A ram's horn, the tip broken off, was blown into; the string of the hunting bow was plucked—the basic methods of sound production and the main categories of instruments had been discovered.

A number of general areas affect the timbre of an instrument. The choice of materials used in its construction influences the sound. A plastic recorder has a brighter sound than a recorder made of wood; a wooden instrument sounds warmer than one made of metal. Some skilled performers even take this idea a step further, preferring a particular type of wood or metal. Recorder players may choose boxwood over maple, and flutists may use instruments made of gold because they believe this metal influences the instrument's tone color.

Though an instrument's construction influences its sound, it is the performer who has the greatest control over timbre. A sound begins with a tonal concept on the part of the performer. That concept is then realized through physical means. Like a fingerprint, a performer's sound is uniquely his or her own. Though the materials remain the same, a piano sounds entirely different in the hands of different performers. The tone-shaping envelope of attack, sustain, and decay will be subtly altered by the individual performer's mental preconception of a piano sound.

All instruments have sound-production elements in common, including

Method of sound production: some means of vibrating the air to produce sound waves.

Resonating chamber: to acoustically amplify the original sound.

Method of pitch alteration: for pitched instruments, some means of producing higher and lower pitches.

From this general beginning, instruments splinter into more definite categories, based on the specific method of sound production, resonation, and pitch alteration.

Percussion Instruments

The clattering of stones, the sound of a stick against a hollow log—the family of percussion instruments was probably the first one to be explored by humans. Percussion instruments are made of a number of different materials and may be of definite or indefinite pitch. They all produce an initial sound in the same general way: They are struck.

Membranophones are percussion instruments with a head (originally of animal skin) stretched tight across a shell, its resonating chamber. The head may be struck with the hand, as in the case of conga or bongo drums, or with a stick, as with the snare drum. In the case of the snare drum, in addition to the head on the top of the drum, a second head is stretched across the bottom of the shell, and gut or steel strands (snares) are placed taut across this second head. The upper head is struck, and the snares on the lower head vibrate sympathetically, producing the characteristic snare drum sound.

Though most membranophones are of indefinite pitch, the best-known members of this category are pitched: the timpani (plural of *timpano*). The heads of these instruments are stretched across a bowl and tuned to specific pitches. A foot-operated pedal is used to change head tension, thereby raising or lowering the pitch of the drum. Early timpani did not have the luxury of this tuning pedal; the pitch was either permanently set or changed only with great difficulty.

Another common type of percussion instrument uses metal or wooden bars in a series, each bar pretuned to a specific pitch. These *keyboard* instruments like xylophone and marimba are so called because the arrangement of their bars is the same as that of the keyboard of the piano.

The timbre of both membranophones and keyboard percussion instruments can be varied by using different materials to construct them. Rosewood is the preferred material for the marimba, for example; other materials do not have the same sound and resonance. Heads for instruments like snare drums and timpani were originally made of skin (cow, goat, etc.). These natural materials are subject to drastic changes depending on the weather and have been replaced in most cases with more consistent synthetic materials.

Timbre is also affected by the choice of beater used in striking the instrument. Xylophone mallets have heads made of either wound yarn or rubber of varying densities. The sound produced when the instrument is struck with yarn mallets is softer and less obtrusive than when struck with rubber mallets. Timpani mallets have felt ends and are made in varying degrees of hardness to provide differences in intensity, clarity, and control.

Another percussion subcategory could be called, for want of a better term, *plate.* Metal instruments like cymbals, gongs, triangles, anvils, brake drum linings, and so on, are found in this category. As with other percussion categories, shades of tone color can be produced depending on where and how hard the instrument is struck and depending on what material is used to strike the instrument. As with other percussion instruments, intensity levels are determined by the strength of the attack, and sound is sustained only through the use of a roll, a quick alternation of left- and right-hand sticks.

Multiple Percussion   Contemporary composers like to experiment by combining various instruments in unique ways. Twentieth-century composers are drawn to the percussion family, a group that had been neglected until this century. Composers and performers now commonly combine percussion instruments of the various subcategories and of definite pitch and indefinite pitch for use in works written for multiple percussion. The most common multiple percussion setup is the drum set, which uses snare drum, kick drum (bass drum), tom-toms, and various cymbals. More adventurous combinations have been used by contemporary composers.

Michael Udow's *Bog Music* is an example of a composition written for multiple percussion, requiring four performers. In the third movement, one instrumentalist plays tuned drums; the other three play multiple percussion setups. This movement includes the following instrumentation:

Soloist:

12 drums: low to high arranged
   in a keyboard configuration
   notated from F-E

Player 1:

5 muted brake drums
Chinese cymbal (suspended)
voice (used to color the attack sounds)

Player 2

2 triangles on 25" timpano

thunder sheet

slapstick

Player 3

5 steel pipes

flexitone

    The performers produce a variety of sounds and combinations of tone colors. One performer uses his of her voice to color the attack of the cymbal, speaking "Cha" clightly softer than the cymbal sound itself, while player 2 uses the pedal of the timpano to alter the sound of the triangles placed on top of the head. Included in these groupings of instruments are domestic found objects such as brake drums and steel pipes.

 Michael Udow, *Bog Music* (3rd mvmt.)

Woodwind Instruments

    All woodwind instruments produce a sound by creating a vibrating column of air. There are three subcategories of woodwinds, grouped by how the initial sound is produced. *Air column* instruments such as the flute and recorder have an edge that is blown across. *Single-reed* instruments like the clarinet and saxophone use a flat reed attached to a mouthpiece to set the air vibrating. Oboes and bassoons have reeds bound together and held between the player's lips; this *double reed* vibrates the air.

    The initial sound is amplified through the body of the instrument. As mentioned, different materials give a different sound. Woodwind instruments were originally made of wood; in some cases, such as the flute and saxophone, metal has replaced this material. Intensity can also be affected by the composition of the body of the instrument, with a wider bore providing more sound than a narrower bore.

    Pitch is changed when the player closes holes in the body of the instrument. This can be done directly, with one hole for each of the player's fingers, or indirectly, through the use of keys that open or close holes. Early versions of woodwind instruments had only seven or eight openings in the instrument and were therefore limited in the number of pitches that could be produced. Modern versions have a wider range of pitches.

    Differences in timbre and in treatment of pitch, intensity, and duration can be heard in the next listening example. You will hear three flute performances: one a traditional Irish air, the second a contemporary "classical" performance, and the last a performance on a Japanese flute (this type of flute is called a *shakuhachi*). The Irish air and the Japanese piece are performed on flutes made of wood, while the "classical" performance is given on a modern metal flute. Each of the flutists has a unique approach to the treatment of the basic elements of music, yet there are some similarities in the performances. Listen for these differences and similarities.

Traditional Irish air, "Sgariunt na
gCompanach" ("The Parting of
Friends")
Bruno Bartolozzi, *Collage for Flute*
Clive Bell, *Disguised as a Silverer of
Mirrors*

Brass Instruments

Brass instruments all produce an initial sound when the performer buzzes into a mouthpiece. The vibrating column of air is then sent through brass tubing (which is often coiled a number of times to produce a more compact instrument). The sound emerges at the end of the tubing, where a flared bell helps project the instrument's sound.

Originally, the only way a performer could alter pitch on a brass instrument was by changing lip tension. The trombone was the first brass instrument to solve this problem, using a slide to lengthen and shorten the tubing of the instrument. Later, valves were added to the trumpet and the horn. These valves open and close combinations of tubing, producing various lengths. Valve combinations in conjunction with changes in lip tension provide a wide range of possible pitches on modern brass instruments.

String Instruments

Strings stretched across a hollow body create a basic string instrument. Instruments in the string family produce a sound when they are plucked or bowed. The bow, a stick with horsehair stretched along its length, can be used only if the instrument has an arched bridge to hold the strings at an angle allowing it to be drawn across one string at a time. Some string instruments, such as the harp and acoustic guitar, are plucked exclusively, while instruments in the violin family can be bowed or plucked.

Pitch is changed on string instruments when the fingers of the left hand press a string against the instrument's fingerboard. The length of the string is shortened, and a higher pitch is produced. Some string instruments, such as the guitar, have metal frets built into the fingerboard (then called a fretboard); when the finger presses down near the fret the fret itself makes contact with the string and raises the pitch. Without a fingerboard, the harp has a number of stationary strings. Pedals allow the harpist to alter the pitch of groups of strings at a time.

Electronic Instruments

For centuries humans have relied on natural materials for making instruments. At first found objects were used as they were; later, alterations were made to these found instruments to customize them. At some point humans began to experiment with the creation and modification of their own instruments, using the basic principles discovered in found instruments. Not until the invention and development of electricity did humans have the ability to produce sounds of their own making.

Electricity and music have had a special relationship since Thomas Edison first introduced his wax cylinder recording device. Since that time recorded music of one form or another has found its way into the majority of American homes.

It did not take long for musicians to recognize the potential of electricity in the area of performance. Electrical amplification of acoustic instruments was the first benefit of this new science. The guitar was the first to take advantage of this boost of power. Now we have electric violins, cellos, and harps that produce special timbres and compete with the ever-increasing level of intensity in today's music.

It was not until the synthesizer was developed, however, that performers and composers were able to create sounds that were truly new. Now a mainstay of the pop, rock, jazz, and even classical music world, the synthesizer took some time to develop. Early versions needed entire rooms to house the necessary equipment. More powerful present-day instruments take up less space than a countertop.

Early synthesizers recreated sound-wave shapes; these *analog synthesizers* started the process at a very basic level, creating simple waveforms, then combining them to create more complex sounds. The analog process provided some interesting electronic sounds but was a rather tedious way to create music. The development of the *digital synthesizer* has made the process much easier.

Digital synthesizers process information in much the same way compact disc players reproduce a recorded sound. In both cases sound waves are analyzed and converted for storage as digital information. Rather than creating a physical piece of magnetic tape, music is stored as a digital code that can be read to re-create the original sound.

Differences Between the Piano and the Synthesizer   At first glance, it would seem that the piano and the synthesizer belong in the same category. A closer look at the way the instruments produce an initial sound and change pitch will show that this is not the case.

The piano is a percussion instrument. Though sound is produced by strings stretched across an acoustic shell, these strings are struck. When a key is depressed an intricate series of levers moves a felt-covered "hammer" to strike the strings (there are usually two to three strings per pitch) of a particular pitch. The harder a key is depressed, the sharper the attack, and the longer the sustain. Pitches of shorter duration are produced if the key is released sooner.

Unlike pianos, synthesizers produce an initial sound through the organization of electrical impulses. Though the synthesizer's keyboard serves the same basic purpose as the piano's (to produce and control sound), it functions in a different way. The keyboard of a synthesizer is actually a series of switches used to signal specific pitch, duration, and sometimes intensity and timbre responses in the "brain" of the instrument. If the keyboard is touch-sensitive, different amounts of finger pressure produce different amounts of intensity. With some synthesizer keyboards, pressing again or wiggling the finger on the depressed key can alter the timbre in predetermined ways.

The piano is a keyboard percussion instrument; the synthesizer is an electronic instrument.

THE CREATIVE PROCESS

Through the selection of different materials, the instrument maker affects the timbre of the instrument as it is created. The performer contributes to the timbre with a conception of tone color and through the manipulation of performance variables—how a string is plucked, the amount of force used blowing into a wind instrument, the choice of fingerings. In turn, the composer can create new and unique tone colors by combining different instruments and by asking the performer to use the instrument in new ways. Asking the percussionist to submerge a gong in water or to scrape a cymbal with a coin are examples of requests made by contemporary composers. Such ability to manipulate timbre can happen only through careful listening and experimentation.

The Creative Assignment in Chapter 1 asked you to create a sound-scene. Working with primitive found objects, you tried to recreate the characteristics of the basic elements of pitch, intensity, and duration, as found in the scene of your choice. Paul Winter gives his own version of a similar scene, with his "Sea Storm." Listen to the ensemble's careful and patient treatment of tension and relaxation in this piece of program music. The gradual building of intensity and rhythmic activity to a climax and the subsequent resolution of tension mimic the pattern that would occur if a ship were stranded at sea while a violent storm passed by.

Winter uses a number of percussion instruments to give the impression of thunder and rumbling storm sounds and also uses cello and organ for sustained swells that give the feeling of the sea at motion. A found object (a trident shell) begins the piece, and a synchronistic thunderclap occurs during taping, allowing nature to make its own contribution to this piece of music.

Listen for ways in which the ensemble uses the elements of pitch, intensity, duration, and timbre to re-create a storm at sea.

    Winter, "Sea Storm"

LISTENING ASSIGNMENT

1. William Schuman's "George Washington Bridge" is a work for concert band inspired by the New York City bridge of the same name. The composer calls his piece an "Impression for Band"—how does he use the basic elements of music and tone color combinations to create a picture of this man-made monument?

2. You will hear a performance of "Improvisation III" by Japanese composer Ryo Noda. Although this work is written for saxophone alone, similarities to the sound of the shakuhachi flute can be heard. As you compare this selection with the earlier listening example *Disguised as a Silverer of Mirrors,* comment on the ways in which the saxophonist creates a shakuhachi sound.

3. Find the following examples heard in previous Listening Assignments. They provide examples of different instruments or categories of instruments.

   Hovhaness, "And God Created Great
     Whales" (strings)
   Mussorgsky/Ravel, "Catacombs" (brass)

Varese, "Octandre" (oboe)
Key, Trio for Recorders (various recorders)
Winston, arr., "Carol of the Bells" (piano)
Debussy, String Quartet
Crumb, *Black Angels: Thirteen Images from
the Dark Land*

If further listening is required to identify instrument categories, use a recording of Benjamin Britten's *Young Person's Guide to the Orchestra.*

CREATIVE ASSIGNMENT

Create an original percussion instrument. Keep in mind that the materials you choose (wood, paper, plastic, paper clips, etc.) affect the timbre to some extent. The material of the beater also affects the tone quality. Experiment with the use of different beaters (including hands) and with striking the instrument in various locations.

Create for your instrument a sound collage of one to two minutes. Your piece can be either program or absolute music. Explore the strengths and weaknesses of your instrument, using changes in the basic elements of music in a creative and coherent way. Strive for clarity of sections, with busy moments leading to cadences, and a gradual development of tension building to a climax. Reach the climax about three-quarters of the way through your composition, then resolve it. Save your creation on your tape.

ECHO PATTERN ASSIGNMENT

Execute the echo patterns for Chapter 3.

JOURNAL ENTRY SUGGESTIONS

Make a note of the different combinations of instruments that you notice in a performance or recording you have recently heard. How many combinations can you identify?

Are there any associative responses that you found yourself having to a particular instrument or combination?

♪♪♪♪♪♪

Rhythmic Organization

The very essence of life is movement.

—Jack London
The Sea Wolf

We have seen how the basic musical elements of pitch, intensity, duration, and timbre are organized. We have also learned something about the way we respond to the physical and emotional aspects of music, and about the associations we attach to the music we hear. As we've learned more about the way musical expression is created and re-created, we have begun to react to music in a more intellectual way as well. Now we need to take a closer look at another basic building block of music: rhythm.

We experience sound even before we are born. Within the protection of our mother's womb we hear the filtered events of the "real" world as well as the sounds of our immediate prenatal environment. We respond to the flow of embryonic fluid, to our mother's breathing, and to her voice. We respond most deeply to the soothing, recurring rhythm of her heartbeat. After birth we continue to respond to the natural and re-created rhythms of the world. In music's natural grouping of pulses and in its basic rhythmic ideas, we are reminded of the comfort of a physical and emotional world where we felt protected and nurtured.

Of the three ways in which we respond to music, our physical–emotional response is most basic. The rhythmic striking of primeval percussion instruments echoes a primitive time and a primal world (perhaps this is why rock music is so powerful for so many). Likewise, the physical element of rhythm forms the foundation of a musical composition. The movement of sound in time, its regular patterns, and the speed of movement form the basic foundation of rhythm. Even when pitches are used to create melody, it is the ever-present rhythmic element we hear most easily. We can imagine music without melody, music that uses rhythm only, but we would find relating to music with no rhythmic organization difficult.

THE MOTIVE

> There is a peculiar thing about repetition in music. Music by and large is almost inconceivable without repetition. It is the rhythmical recurrence of a motivic pattern that provides the unifying undercurrent of sections, at least, if not of whole movements. Besides, we welcome the recurrence of themes as another means of unification and formal support to musical structure. . . . No motif is too small, too insignificant, too negligible to promote, not only construction and movement, but inspiration itself. . . .

> —Ernst Toch
> *The Shaping Forces of Music*

Ernst Toch, a composer himself, writes about the use of the motive in music. A *motive,* or *motif,* is a small musical idea that serves as a figurative brick in the construction of a piece of music. It is the shortest musical idea that can stand on its own. As we have already discovered, for this idea to be without rhythmic impulse would be impossible. Indeed, for some composers, the rhythm of the idea is most important.

The germinating possibilities of an entire composition can sometimes be held in the small kernel of a rhythm. This is the case with the first movement of Ludwig van Beethoven's Symphony No. 5. The motive is introduced a few times, with a pause between statements and a change in pitch. Beethoven then piles one statement of the motive on another. Pitch relationships may vary, but the rhythm of the motive stays the same; the rhythmic drive of the entire movement is found in this one short idea.

Beethoven, Symphony No. 5 (portion of 1st mvmt.)

Another symphony of Beethoven's, the last he was to write, uses a rhythmic motive for an entire movement. The scherzo movement of the Symphony No. 9 is based on one rhythmic motive. This motive is said to have come to the composer "in a flash" as he stepped out of the darkness and into the light. This idea was the first theme of the entire symphony that was put on paper. Listen for ways in which Beethoven keeps our interest, even while he uses and reuses just one motive. With this movement Beethoven demonstrates that "no motif is too small, too insignificant, too negligible to promote, not only construction and movement, but inspiration itself."

    Beethoven, Symphony No. 9 (portion of
                          2nd mvmt.)

Bob James, a jazz musician, was so intrigued with Beethoven's scherzo that he arranged this movement for synthesizers, horns, and a rhythm section. Steve Gadd, a well-known studio drummer, performed on the arrangement and made a personal, creative contribution as well.

Gadd improvised a solo that uses the basic rhythmic motive of the scherzo to the utmost. His use of the drum set as a multiple-percussion instrument is effectively demonstrated in the presentation of the motive on kick drum, snare drum, tom-tom, and cymbals. Gadd's organization of rhythmic ideas was so compelling that James arranged melodic horn and synthesizer parts to accompany Gadd's solo. In Gadd's improvisation, James heard an underlying melodic scheme, a melodic organization of rhythm. It is not uncommon for musicians in the studio to make numerous attempts at recording a part, doing a number of "takes." Gadd's solo was recorded in one "take"—we hear a recording of a live, uninterrupted improvisation performed in one sitting. His solo imspired the melodic accompaniment later added by James, with varied presentations of the basic scherzo motive.

THE SPECIFIC ORGANIZATION OF RHYTHM

In the examples we have just heard, we can identify basic rhythmic motives and hear repetitions of ideas, but there are other rhythmic elements at work. Even while these specific rhythmic motives are being presented and developed, a more general rhythmic concept is in evidence. In these examples, and in most music, two important underlying rhythmic elements can be found, the two components of rhythm: meter and tempo.

Meter

Meter is used to describe the grouping of underlying rhythmic pulses in music. No matter what type of rhythmic ideas are presented, you will be able to simplify the rhythmic organization—you will be able to tap your foot to a basic underlying pulse. The majority of music we hear uses one of two repeating patterns: an underlying pulse of two or of three.

Most pop and rock music has an underlying pulse of two. Marches like "The Stars and Stripes Forever" have a meter of two, probably to make it easier for people with two feet to march to the music. Music that groups underlying pulses into sets of two is said to have a *duple meter*. The first Beethoven example we heard (the Symphony No. 5 excerpt) was in a duple meter; like a march we could feel a pulse of one, two, one, two, and so on, throughout most of the music. Some other previous listening examples that show a duple meter are the following:

Key, Trio for Recorders (from Chapter 1
    Listening Assignment)
Debussy, String Quartet (from Chapter 2
    Listening Assignment)

Some music demonstrates a pulse grouping of three, a *triple meter*. The Beethoven scherzo is in triple meter, with the underlying pulses moving very quickly. In fact, Beethoven developed the scherzo, with its very fast triple meter, as a more exciting alternative to the traditional minuet and trio movement, which uses a slower triple meter.

"The Star-Spangled Banner" is another example of music in a triple meter. If you tap out a basic pulse while you sing, you will feel the music follow the rhythm of the text, setting up a recurring pattern of three. You might also notice that the words *see* and *light* are held longer than the other words—a demonstration of short sections of movement and rest giving rhythmic direction to the text. If you were to sing the national anthem, the first stress point, the true beginning of the feeling of pulse, would be on the word *say*. The words that occur on the first pulse of each grouping of three are italicized: (O) *Say,* can you *see,* by the *dawn's* early *light . . .*

The waltz, a dance form, uses a triple meter. If music you hear sounds like the "Blue Danube" waltz, the piece is in a meter of three. Previous listening examples that demonstrate a triple meter include:

Traditional, arr. Winston, "Carol of the
    Bells" (from Chapter 2 Listening Assignment)
Traditional, arr. Winston, "The Holly and
    the Ivy" (from Chapter 2 Listening Assignment)

It is important to remember that the meter of a piece of music is not necessarily felt in its rhythmic activity. There can be a flurry of pitches, but there will still be a pulse, a steady heartbeat that underlies the rhythms themselves. To identify the meter of a piece, you must feel that underlying heartbeat.

Some music is composed in meters that use a combination of two and three. A meter of five, seven, or another combination of twos and threes is called a *complex meter*. Even when the grouping of pulses is more complex, however, there are still subgroupings of two and three. A meter of five divides into two plus three or three plus two; a meter of seven is grouped two plus two plus three, three plus two plus two, or two plus three plus two. This same arrangement of twos and threes occurs with other "odd" meters like nine or eleven. Though these meters are not common in our musical vocabulary, other cultures seem to be more comfortable with them. Some countries even use complex meters like five and seven for dances.

Though it has been pointed out that rhythm is basic to almost all music, there are times when a composer or performer may wish to use rhythm in a freer way. A melody or a vocal text may require a changing meter to allow the music to follow the rhythms of the text (or of the composer's imagination). If you set one of the poems in the Creative Assignment in Chapter 2 to music, you probably ended up following this procedure, even if you didn't realize it at the time. Some of the listening examples used in previous chapters show a very flexible or nonexistent meter. The Japanese shakuhachi flute improvisation and the Ryo Noda work for saxophone ("Improvisation III"), because they are improvisations, don't have a strict sense of meter. Refer to these previous examples to hear how composers work with a free sense of rhythm.

Tempo

Tempo refers to the speed at which the underlying pulses are felt to be moving. As with meter, the frequency of pitches is not necessarily related to tempo. The music can be very busy but with a slow underlying pulse. Conversely, pitches of longer duration can be accompanied by a quicker pattern of underlying pulses.

"Classical" music has a highly developed hierarchy of tempos, with a number of variations on basic speeds. Classical composers often use the musician's international language of Italian to indicate the tempo of a composition:

adagio	very slow
andante	walking pace
moderato	moderate
allegro	lively (fast)
presto	very fast

These are some of the Italian terms a composer might use at the beginning of a piece and whenever the tempo changes. Variations of these basic terms can be used to indicate a subtler speed, as with allegretto (somewhat fast). Terms can be even further modified, as with *allegro ma non troppo* (fast, but not too). Composers and performers recognize that tempo is an important part of the character of a piece and that more than speed is implied with a tempo indication. *Un poco Allegretto e grazioso* (a little bit fast and graceful) tries to indicate not only the tempo desired but the character of the music as well.

Refer to previous listening examples that demonstrate various tempos and meters:

Winter, "Ocean Dream" (from Chapter 1
    Listening Example)
allegro—triple meter

Mendelssohn, "Dance of the Clowns," *Midsummer
    Night's Dream* (from Chapter 1 Listening Assignment)
allegro—duple meter

Key, Trio for Recorders (from Chapter 1
    Listening Assignment)
allegro—duple meter

THE CREATIVE PROCESS

The inherent musical qualities and melodic capabilities of rhythm can be explored during the composition process. Even instruments of indefinite pitch can be used in a musical way and can create the impression of general pitch change. In the following recorded example, through careful manipulation of the head and the beater, an Irish bodhran (a hand-held drum) can follow the basic contours of a melody that it accompanies.

Traditional Irish, "Heuliadenn Toniou
    Breizh-Izel"

Timpani were first used in conjunction with trumpets, maintaining the historical pairing of the two. In orchestral compositions, the timpani form an underlying rhythmic and melodic support for the trumpet.

Franz Joseph Haydn, Symphony No. 104
    (portion of 1st mvmt.)

Percussion instruments can be used on their own as well. John Cage has written a piece for four performers, each on a wood block. He uses a rhythmic ostinato in each part to create unity and organization. An *ostinato* is a short pattern that is repeated continuously throughout a composition or a section. In Cage's piece the various introductions of solo ostinati and their combinations bring variety and unity to the piece.

Cage, *Amores*

LISTENING ASSIGNMENT

A. Identify the meter of each example as *duple* or *triple*.

   1.
   2.
   3.

B. Identify the tempo of each selection as moderate, fast, or very fast, and then provide the proper Italian term.

   1.
   2.
   3.

CREATIVE ASSIGNMENT

You will be asked to work together with other members of the class in a small group. Each member of the group will use his or her homemade percussion instrument, contributing to a group multiple-percussion ensemble. Your instructor will provide specific rhythmic motives for you to use as an ensemble, developing a group composition thirty seconds to one minute in length.

Appoint one person leader/conductor of the ensemble. This person will coordinate instrument use and oversee use of motives and the general development of the piece. As an ensemble, you should explore the timbre possibilities of each instrument as well as instruments in combination, and decide on ideas of musical development. Decide how you will use rhythmic material and instrument combinations to create an ensemble piece that demonstrates the qualities of a good composition. In your piece, do not be concerned with pitch, but employ changes in intensity, duration, and timbre. The leader/conductor will serve as a guide for entrances, cutoffs, and changes in intensity. You will be asked to perform your creation and preserve it on tape.

ECHO PATTERN ASSIGNMENT

Perform Chapter 4 echo patterns 1 through 8.

JOURNAL ENTRY SUGGESTIONS

Discuss the power of rhythm and its impact on you as you listen to a piece of music with strong rhythms.

Some forms of "rap" music are created primarily of rhythms. Is this a legitimate form of music? Why or why not? (You might wish to refer to your definition of *music* if you completed the first suggested Journal Entry in Chapter 1.)

♪♪♪♪♪♪

Melodic Organization

We respond easily to the physical sensation of rhythm, yet music's melody receives our most conscious attention. Many of us like to leave a performance singing melodies from selections we have heard. Often we judge the merit of a piece of music on the one criterion "Does it have singable melodies?" Some twentieth-century composers (and some rap performers) downplay the role of melody in their works and argue against such a limiting statement. They insist that melody is not a necessary ingredient and that good works that concentrate on the elements of rhythm and timbre can be created. Some may agree with this statement, but it is still true that most of us relate more easily to music that contains melodies.

A *melody* is a series of pitches that form a coherent unit. During the process of its presentation a good melody will develop tension, reach a climax, and resolve. As it follows this general outline it combines repetition of ideas (to help us remember melodic motives) with variety of material (to hold our interest).

Rhythm plays an important role in the development of melodies. Changing lengths of duration provide a sense of motion; cadences contribute to this feeling with prominent resting points. This creation of tension and relaxation combines with the balanced presentation of ideas to delineate a melody's beginning, development, and end.

MELODIC CONTOUR

Melodies come in a variety of shapes and sizes. Some melodies are very short; others are long. Melodies tend to take on a descending, ascending, arch, or wave contour, or shape; or they may take on any combination of these shapes.

Descending

A melody that begins on a higher pitch then moves down a series of pitches to end at a lower point has a descending contour. The Christmas carol "Joy to the World" is an example of a melody that follows this contour.

Ex. 5.1

Ascending

The opposite of descending. The melody begins on a low pitch then rises through a series of pitches to a higher point.

Ex. 5.2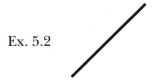

Arch

A combined ascending and descending contour. An arch melody begins on a low pitch and gradually rises to climax on a higher pitch, then descends again. Because of its built-in development of musical tension and relaxation of tension, this is a common contour.

Ex. 5.3

Wave

A modified arch that has some shorter arches, or waves, built in.

Ex. 5.4

"Irish Tune from County Derry" (also known as "Danny Boy") follows this contour, with its series of short waves. The middle waves bring the melody to a climax, and a short wave brings the melody back down. This melody is also a good example of conjunct melodic motion. *Conjunct* melodies move smoothly from one pitch to the next, with few jumps between pitches. This type of melody is more easily assimilated by the ear than a melody that is disjunct. A *disjunct* melody jumps from one pitch to the next in an angular fashion. A good melody shows some of both; it is never a good idea to use one type of motion exclusively. A good conjunct melody avoids boredom with some well-placed "bold leaps"; disjunct melodies are easier to hear if they have sections of conjunct motion. "Irish Tune from County Derry" makes good use not only of a wave contour but of conjunct and disjunct motion as well. Though we may be used to hearing this selection with lyrics, the "Irish Tune from County Derry" is a traditional Irish air (similar to "The Parting of Friends," heard in Chapter 3). Lyrics were not added until the late 1800s. Hearing this beautiful Irish melody without lyrics can help us appreciate the melodic contours, the use of conjunct and disjunct motion, and the development of musical ideas found in this piece.

Traditional Irish air, arr. Percy Grainger,
"Irish Tune from County Derry"

Melodies often use one or more of these basic melodic contours. When listening for melodic contours, it is important to go for the "small" picture. Melodies use more than one contour; rather than hearing just one, you might find that careful analysis reveals a series of melodic contours at work. Several listening examples can be used to identify examples of different contours. Listen for the type of contour each uses, then turn to page 47 for the correct answers. Remember that these examples may use more than one type of contour.

1. Winter, "Ocean Dream" (from Chapter 1)
2. Key, Trio for Recorders (from Chapter 1 Listening Assignment)
3. Franz Schubert, "Gute Nacht," from *Die Winterreise* (from Chapter 4 Listening Assignment)
4. Beethoven, Symphony No. 6 (1st mvmt.) (from Chapter 4 Listening Assignment)

THE CREATIVE PROCESS

The concepts of repetition and variety have been discussed before. Reaching a balance between these two extremes is especially important when writing melodies. Sounds pass, never to be heard again; the composer must help the listener remember important melodic ideas so that the listener can make sense of the music. The repetition of melodies and of basic motives plays an important role in this process.

We have been introduced to the concept of the motive as a building block of music. Good melodies use short motives as basic material. These short ideas are combined to form musical *phrases*. Two or more phrases then combine to create a *period*. *Cadences* are used to separate each of these sections, with a *final cadence* (one that has a stronger sense of "coming home") bringing the melody to a rest.

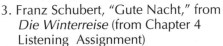

Identify the types of melodic contours used in two selections you enjoy listening to.

PERFORMANCE ASSIGNMENT

Perform each of the sound collages on the next page. Interpret the graphic notation in a creative and musical way, developing a "vocabulary" of sounds to match the different graphic ideas. Use voice or an instrument to give a representation of the changes in basic elements and melodic contours that seem to be suggested in each sound collage.

1.

2.

CREATIVE ASSIGNMENT

Create an original melody for voice alone or for an instrument of your choice (traditional or found). When you are satisfied with the results, record your melody on your Creative-Assignment tape.

Once you have recorded your melody, turn the page and answer the questions on it.

Analyze your melody and answer the following questions:

1. What types of melodic contours did you use?

2. How did you use rhythmic and pitch changes to create and resolve tension?

3. Does your melody have a strong final cadence, with a sense of "coming home"?

4. If you could change anything about your melody, what would you change? How and why?

Save your first recorded melody but also create a revised version that explores changes in the areas discussed above. When you have recorded your second version, devise and use a graphic system of notation that provides a general reminder of changes in the basic elements of music that occur in your melody. Your notation may be somewhat like the Performance Assignment examples on the previous page, but should give a more definite indication of changes. Do not use traditional notation; be imaginative in creating your own visual representation, which could serve as a reminder for future performances.

JOURNAL ENTRY SUGGESTIONS

Can you recall the sound of a favorite melody? Is the melody memorable because of associative connections or because of its own unique qualities?

Can you recall a melody without accompanying lyrics? Does the character of a melody change if you hear it without lyrics? How?

_____

_____

_____

_____

_____

_____

_____

_____

_____

_____

_____

_____

_____

_____

_____

_____

_____

Answers to Listening Examples on page 44   1. wave   2. ascending wave, descending
3. descending   4. wave

♪♪♪♪♪♪

CHAPTER 6

Texture

The presentation of a coherent series of pitches gives music its melody. This horizontal aspect of music combines with the vertical to provide music's texture. Just as the warp and woof of a fabric can be plain or patterned, the texture of music can be simple or complex.

MONOPHONIC TEXTURE

The Creative Assignment in Chapter 2 asked you to set a poem to music, using only your voice. Unless you overdubbed a second vocal part, your final composition consisted of just one melodic part. Though the melodies you created may have varied during the course of your composition, the texture remained the same, following one plane. When the performers are all singing or playing just one melodic part, the simplest of textures is created: *monophonic* (one sound).

Much Western classical music has its roots in the monophonic chants of the Christian church, themselves descendants of Judaic monophonic melodies. The following listening example is such a melody.

The text of the "Dies Irae" is attributed to Thomas of Celano, who died about 1250. The "Dies Irae" was officially included in the Catholic church's Requiem (mass for the dead) in the sixteenth century. As with other chants, this one is sung monophonically. Though there may be a number of singers, they all sing the same part, producing a texture of just one melodic line.

    Chant, "Dies Irae"

The "Dies Irae" has been used for its associative connections in a number of compositions. In a Chapter 2 Listening Assignment we heard a section of George Crumb's *Black Angels*. The particular excerpt is called "Danse Macabre," from the first section of Crumb's piece. This first section portrays the first of three journeys of the soul and is called "Departures" (fall from grace). Inspired by the Vietnam War, Crumb quotes a number of compositions in this work, including the "Dies Irae." We hear this melody played pizzicato first, then as high-pitched bowed notes with accompanying whistles.

Perhaps the best-known quotation of the "Dies Irae" theme is found in Hector Berlioz's work for orchestra, *Symphonie fantastique*. Written in 1830, *Symphonie fantastique* is a programmatic work. The composition depicts the life and love of a young artist (Berlioz himself) who has fallen in love. He sees his beloved everywhere and is obsessed with thoughts of her. He notices her at a ball (second movement) and thinks of her while he is in the countryside (third movement). In a fit of rage because she will not notice him, the artist kills her, and finds himself being led to the scaffold (fourth movement). In the fifth and final movement of the piece, "The Witches' Sabbath," the artist is tortured beyond the grave by demons, witches, and the distorted image of his beloved. It is this movement that makes use of the "Dies Irae" theme.

As with the examples discussed in Chapter 2 (Sting's "Russians" and the film *Platoon*), *Symphonie fantastique* counts on the associative responses of the listener. The "Dies Irae," which speaks of Judgment Day, has a melody and message that would have been familiar to Berlioz's listeners. Berlioz introduces this theme in its original monophonic texture. The tubas, the lowest-pitched instruments of the brass family, serve either as monks or as a reminder of the depths of hell.

    Berlioz, *Symphonie fantastique* (5th mvmt.)

Early church music favored monophonic texture, and an orchestral piece like *Symphonie fantastique* can use this same texture to evoke associative responses from the listener. The church is not the only place where we find this texture, however. Vocal and instrumental folk musicians favor music with a monophonic texture. In Chapter 3 we heard an Irish air

("The Parting of Friends") that used this texture. Our shakuhachi flute example in the same chapter also had a monophonic texture. Robbie O'Connell's contemporary composition "Two Nations" (heard in Chapter 2) captures the flavor of a traditional song with its use of a monophonic texture.

POLYPHONIC TEXTURE

A more complex texture is created when more than one melody is heard at the same time. A round is a good example of a piece of music that uses this type of texture. Monophonic at first, a song like "Row, Row, Row Your Boat," with its separate, overlapping entrances, creates a *polyphonic* texture—more than one melody is heard at the same time.

Though polyphonic texture is more easily produced by separate vocalists or instrumentalists performing together, it is possible for this texture to be produced on one instrument. A keyboard player has the perfect opportunity to create two independent parts on one instrument, and many polyphonic works or sections of works have been written for keyboard instruments. We heard a polyphonic work, a fugue by Bach, in Listening Assignment B2 in Chapter 4. This work was performed on a guitarlike instrument, the lute. Refer to this example if you would like to hear an instrumental example of polyphonic texture.

Bach, Fugue, from Prelude, Fugue, and
Allegro in E♭ Major (from Chapter 4)

It is important to note that the special sound of polyphonic music is created through the complementary use of independent melodic lines. If we were to separate the parts of a polyphonic composition or section, each part could stand on its own as a melody. Played or sung together, these concurrent melodies produce music with a polyphonic texture.

HOMOPHONIC TEXTURE

So far, we have dealt with music that uses melody to produce monophonic or polyphonic texture. More commonly, music is made of melody and harmony. *Harmony* is the vertical aspect of music created when chords are used. *Chords* are created when three or more pitches are sounded simultaneously. Composers move from one chord to another to create harmonic progressions. When this harmony is used in conjunction with melody, music with a *homophonic* texture is the result. The next listening example demonstrates this.

Anatol Liadov, arr. J. Michael Leonard, Prelude,
Op. 31, No. 2

In this arrangement for alto saxophone and piano, the piano sometimes has melodic lines of its own, but for the most part it acts as an accompaniment to the soloist. Because harmony serves as a background and
moves separately from the melody, the texture created in this piece is
called *accompanied* homophonic texture. Just as often, though, melody and
harmony move together; chords are sung or played in the same rhythm as
the melody, creating a *choral* homophonic texture. Randall Thompson uses
this specific type of texture in "Stopping by Woods on a Snowy Evening,"
one of the Robert Frost poems he sets to music in *Frostiana.*

Thompson, "Stopping by Woods on a Snowy Evening"

Though this specific type of homophonic texture is called choral, it is
not used exclusively in vocal music. Instrumental music too can apply this
texture to great effect.

THE CREATIVE PROCESS

As with other elements of music, texture changes during the course of a
composition to provide variety and interest. A composer might begin with
a monophonic texture, then use a section of polyphonic texture to create
tension, and finally bring ideas together in a homophonic statement.
Alternatively, a composer might have two independent melodic lines giving
a sense of polyphony and still use chordal accompaniment to give an overall impression of homophonic texture. As with the use of different types of
intensity changes, we might find more than one type of texture being used
at once in a composition.

Just as a composer works with different levels of pitch, intensity, and
duration, and will vary the use of instruments in a work, texture is used as a
tool for artistic expression. Review the following listening examples and
Listening Assignments, and determine which types of texture are being
used.

1. Key, Trio for Recorders (from Chapter 1)
2. Traditional, "The Parting of Friends" (from Chapter 3)
3. Schuman, "George Washington Bridge"
   (from Chapter 3)

4. Noda, "Improvisation III" (from Chapter 3)
5. Beethoven, Symphony No. 9 (from Chapter 4)
6. Haydn, Symphony No. 104 (from Chapter 4)
7. Traditional, "Irish Tune from County Derry" (from Chapter 5)

See page 54 for answers.

Sometimes a composer uses specific textures to fit the meaning of the music or the text. In Stephanie Caron's setting of "The Two-Headed Calf," how do changes in texture help convey the mood of the poem and emphasize specific ideas of the text?

   Caron/Gilpin, "The Two-Headed Calf"

The use of texture to convey the meaning of the text is one example of tone painting in music. *Tone painting* involves the use of various techniques to portray the text in music. Handel's "Hallelujah" chorus uses texture and other musical elements to create a "picture" of the words. The timbre of the trumpet is used (as we saw in Chapter 3) to provide an associative connection with royalty. This gives "King of Kings" and "Lord of Lords" a strong visual and aural image. Other lines in the text are highlighted through the use of texture as well as melodic contour. "For the Lord God omnipotent reigneth" is the first time in the chorus where monophonic texture is used. Why did Handel choose this texture for this line of text? What word is emphasized in this line, and how does the melody help portray its meaning? At this point, and throughout the "Hallelujah" chorus, Handel uses changes in pitch, intensity, timbre, and texture to emphasize the meaning of the text.

   Handel, "Hallelujah" chorus (from the *Messiah*)

LISTENING ASSIGNMENT

Complete the following Listening Guide for a short selection of your choice. Submit a tape of your selection along with the completed Listening Guide.

Title:

Timbre (list instruments used):

Types of intensity changes (choose one or more):

Terraced _____   Sudden _____   Gradual _____

Meter:

Duple _____   Triple _____   Other_____

Tempo:

Adagio _____   Andante _____   Moderato _____   Allegro _____   Presto _____

Predominate Texture:

Monophonic _____   Polyphonic _____

Accompanied homophonic _____   Choral homophonic _____

JOURNAL ENTRY SUGGESTIONS

You have been appointed by the federal government to serve on a special Smithsonian Institute Committee. As a member of this committee, it will be your responsibility to determine which music will be placed in the Smithsonian archives. Due to the present financial situation, you can include only six CDs per year. What criteria would you use to decide which artists and performances will be included?

Texture seems to have "progressed" historically from monophonic to polyphonic to homophonic. Does this seem to you to be a true "progression" of development? Why or why not?

If you are familiar with music of another culture, discuss the uses of texture in this music.

_____

_____

_____

_____

_____

_____

Answers to Listening Examples on pages 51–52 1. Monophonic, polyphonic
2. Monophonic 3. Homophonic 4. Monophonic 5. Polyphonic
6. Homophonic 7. Homophonic

♪♪♪♪♪♪

CHAPTER 7

Form

In trying to better understand how music is created and how we listen to it, we have concentrated on the finer details. With our discussion of rhythm, melody, and texture we have begun to think in broader terms about how music works. This chapter continues in that vein, as we look at the overall picture of music and begin to recognize the ways in which elements are combined and repetition and variety balanced. We will work with music's larger scope of material, with its overall form.

SONG FORMS

The simplest of forms in music are called *song forms*. These forms have either two or three varying sections. Like all forms, these use motives in combination to create themes. The use of cadences outlines the larger sections of these song forms, with final cadences signaling the end of a section. In some ways, we can draw an analogy between musical form and the structure of sentences and paragraphs.

As I write down my thoughts, I am using words. Letters of the alphabet are placed together to form these most basic of written symbols. In music, we use a version of letters (pitches) to create words (motives). Words are placed together to form phrases, with the end of a sentence signaled by a period. These same terms, *phrase* and *period*, are used to delineate the next level of structure in music. The final cadence of a period provides us with the first of our two or three sections of a song form.

The simplest of song forms uses motives to create short themes. Themes combine to form phrases, and two or more phrases create a period, which gives us an A section. The contrasting B section uses different melodic material and again is signaled by a final cadence:

Ex. 7.1

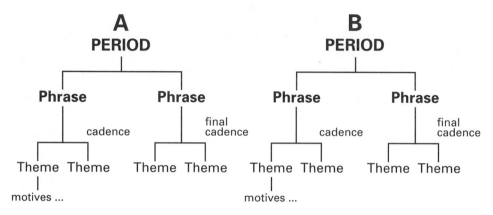

This two-part form is the most basic of song forms. The diagram above is a general guide that could be varied somewhat, depending on the selection. The number of themes or phrases can vary, though even groupings of two or four are common. With a two-part form, there are always two clear sections (periods), with a final cadence for each.

"Irish Tune from County Derry," heard in Chapter 5, is in A–B form. Refer to this example to hear this *binary* form.

 Traditional Irish air, "Irish Tune from County Derry" (from Chapter 5)

A second song form is in three parts. This *ternary* form has an A section, a contrasting B section, then a return to the A material, either verbatim, or varied. "Simple Gifts" demonstrates this song form.

 Traditional, arr. Copland, "Simple Gifts"

Though these basic forms are called song forms, they are not limited to vocal music. Much of the world's vocal and instrumental music uses the basic structure of a song form to provide coherence. A binary or ternary form allows for the most basic alternation of material, but there are a number of other possibilities for structuring music.

RONDO

Because repetition and variety are both equally important in music, another common type of form is the *rondo,* which has a returning A section alternating with varying material between. A–B–A–C–A is a common version of this form, though extended variations of the rondo form may be used. Rondo form is used more in instrumental than in vocal music, but can still have a song form feeling to it. Indeed, rondo form is really an extended type of song form, using a returning A section with varying material between.

Beethoven, *Pathetique* Sonata (2nd mvmt.)

THEME AND VARIATIONS

Perhaps the ultimate balance between repetition and variety is found in the *theme and variations* form. A composition that uses this form presents a basic melody, called the theme. After the presentation of the theme, various versions of it are presented. Rhythm, melody, timbre, texture, and harmony are all areas of possible change. Some variations might sound a good deal like the original theme; others need to be scrutinized carefully to find a connection with the main idea. The example given shows some of the possible variations on a very common theme.

Matthias Friederich, "Happy Birthday" Variations

The variations on this theme imitate the style of certain periods or composers. Only some of the fourteen variations are presented on the taped example. After the theme is stated, a variation that gives the monophonic setting of a chant is heard. A Mozart variation imitates the style of that famous composer, and an Elgar variation can be identified by the musical quotation of one of Elgar's *Pomp and Circumstance* marches. A Dixieland variation provides a change in timbre, with the soprano recorder player switching to sopranino recorder. This high recorder performs Dixieland-style patterns while the alto recorder gives a version of the melody and the tenor recorder provides a bass line. After this Dixieland variation, a statement of the original theme reminds us of the basic melodic material on which the set of variations is based.

THE CREATIVE PROCESS

Form deals with the concept of repetition and variety on a larger scale. This concept can be seen at work in a smaller way as well, contributing to the structure of a piece of music. Melodies may show different types of repetition within phrases and periods. If there is a repetition of melody, with little change, we call this an *exact repetition* of material. If the same melodic contour is used for the repetition of the melody, with the second part of the phrase starting on a different pitch, a sequence is being used, and is called a *sequential repetition*. This type of repetition is common as a structural element in music and serves as a miniform within the larger form of the piece.

Most of us work better when we are given specific guidelines and boundaries. The sonnet is a very structured poetic form; it requires great skill and artistry to produce an aesthetically pleasing work when dealing with the limitations of this form. And yet these strict limitations can enhance the creative process. The same is true for the composer of music. Igor Stravinsky, in *Poetics of Music,* discusses this:

> My freedom will be so much the greater and more meaningful the more narrowly I limit my field of action and the more I surround myself with obstacles. Whatever diminishes constraint, diminishes strength. The more constraints one imposes, the more one frees one's self of the chains that shackle the spirit.

Structure and limitations provide freedom during the creative process. Feeling like you can do whatever you want can be a very daunting experience, while setting specific guidelines and working within them can let the creative mind work with greater freedom. Though it may seem to be a paradox, this can be the case for many composers.

A great number of possibilities are available to composers when structuring music. Some of these have been discussed in this chapter, but even these basic structural elements can be varied. Composers are always searching for ways to organize their material in new and creative ways.

LISTENING ASSIGNMENT

Identify the basic form of two selections you enjoy listening to.

CREATIVE ASSIGNMENT

This chapter has dealt with the basic elements of form as applied to melodic music. These same structural principles can also be applied to rhythm.

Choose a previous rhythmic creation to use as source material for this assignment. Decide on a song form (binary or ternary) for your new piece. Work with your rhythmic material so that you have clear rhythmic phrases and periods, with a final cadence signaling the end of the A section. Create a contrasting B section that is clearly different from the first section. If you are working with a ternary form, return to the A material, either as originally stated, or varied. Save your work on your Creative-Assignment tape.

JOURNAL ENTRY SUGGESTIONS

Comment on Stravinsky's view of artistic freedom, as expressed in *Poetics of Music*.

The artist provides himself or herself with self-constraints, even if they are not as constraining as Stravinsky's. Should others, such as the federal government, be allowed to decide limits of artistic expression? Why or why not?

Aside from the ideas discussed in this chapter, what other elements in music provide it with structure?

PART TWO

CHAPTER 8

♪♪♪♪♪♪

Introduction to Notation

In many of the world's cultures, music is learned aurally, handed down from performer to performer, from one generation to the next. Classical music of the Western world, however, has depended on written notation since the end of medieval times. Used first simply as a mnemonic device for singers, Western notation has developed to the point where it now requires some understanding of the process for one to properly interpret its message.

With an introduction to basic Italian tempo markings you have already begun to deal with the vocabulary of traditional Western musical notation. An indication of the tempo of the music is often one of the first instructions to be seen on the printed page. The other important piece of information given at the beginning of a composition tells the performer the meter of the piece. "Allegro:2" would be a logical way to show that the composition is quick and in a duple meter. We will see that composers have even more specific ways of indicating meter and tempo.

In addition to tempo and meter, notation must deal with other basic elements of music. Pitch, intensity, and duration changes must be shown. Timbre changes, both those required of individual performers and those involving various combinations of instruments, must be made clear. The task of preserving on paper the combinations of sounds and ideas that were in the composer's aural imagination is a difficult one. Pitch-specific notation, with its many symbols and indications, is used in an effort to make the composer's wishes clearly known and continues to evolve in keeping with the developments of music itself.

THE DEVELOPMENT OF NOTATION

Pitch

Early forms of notation gave only a general indication of pitch. Because pitches tended to be grouped in small numbers, forming specific patterns (like the echo patterns you've been working with), small "squiggles" served as reminders of these pitch clusters. The "Dies Irae" heard in Chapter 6 might have had a few of these squiggles placed over the text. This *chironomic* notation was the earliest type of neumatic notation (the notational markings were called *neumes*) and was the only reminder needed to jog the memory of a forgetful monk. Chironomic notation did not indicate specific pitches, just general accents and melodic contours. The director of a choir helped interpret these signs through the use of special hand signals. The signs used were similar to the following:

Ex. 8.1

Eventually the vocabulary of melodic patterns became too complex for this system. As polyphonic music came to the forefront, a more specific system of neumatic notation was needed. Chironomy gave way to more specific neumatic notation, which indicated single pitches or groups of pitches. The next refinement in the system came with the development of a reference pitch that was named and indicated with a line.

Ex. 8.2

Anytime a neume struck the line, the singer knew that an F was to be sung. Neumes placed above the line indicated a higher pitch; those positioned below the line told the performer that the pitch needed to be lower than F.

As time went on, more and more lines were added, providing reference points for a greater number of pitches. The *staff,* as this system of lines and spaces came to be known, eventually progressed to the point where it became cumbersome.

Ex. 8.3

This eleven-line staff was separated into two five-line staves with an imaginary line shared between them. A letter was used at the beginning of each staff to indicate the reference pitch and its location. The lower staff used the original F, and the upper staff a higher G. The original Latin letters of $\mathcal{F}$ and $\mathcal{C}$ gradually evolved into the modern *F clef* and *G clef.* The combination of this *bass clef staff* and *treble clef staff,* as they are also known, survives as our *grand staff.*

Ex. 8.4

Duration

As with pitches, the performance of rhythms was limited at first to groupings of recurring patterns. Certain rhythmic modes were used in early Western music. Rhythmic modes were learned in much the same way that you have learned rhythms, through the mastery of basic patterns. You know what ♩ ♪♪ ♩ ♩ (*du du de du*) sounds like because you associate the symbols with a specific rhythmic pattern and use rhythmic syllables to help you recall the specific sound and feeling of the pattern. Early Western church music had similar sets of rhythmic patterns that would have been mastered in much the same way by the performers of the time.

Eventually, music moved away from the system of rhythmic modes, and the vocabulary of rhythms increased. We will learn more about rhythmic notation in future chapters.

Intensity

Intensity indications came later in the historical development of notation. At first, changes in intensity were limited to changes in instrumental or vocal numbers. Instruments themselves had a narrow range of intensity levels; a louder intensity level required more instruments, and a softer level used fewer instruments. Terraced intensity changes were employed. Such changes did not require notation; they were built into the music. As instruments' ability to produce a wide variety of intensity levels developed (in the early 1700s), indications for intensity became necessary. Gradual and sudden changes were possible and needed to be notated.

As with tempo markings, basic intensity indications, called *dynamic markings,* used Italian terms and abbreviations to indicate different *dynamics,* or levels of intensity.

Ex. 8.5	*p*	the abbreviation for *piano* (soft)
	f	the abbreviation for *forte* (loud)

Modifications of these two basic terms provide us with a wide-ranging vocabulary of dynamic markings. These include

	pp	*pianissimo*	(very soft)
	p	*piano*	(soft)
Ex. 8.6	*mp*	*mezzopiano*	(medium soft)
	mf	*mezzoforte*	(medium loud)
	f	*forte*	(loud)
	ff	*fortissimo*	(very loud)

Further modifications are possible, especially for dramatic effect. The abbreviation *pppppp* is used by Tchaikovsky in his Symphony No. 6 more to make a point than to demand a specific intensity level.

Gradual changes in intensity may be shown graphically:

Ex. 8.7

become louder

become softer

or with Italian terms or abbreviations:

Ex. 8.8

cresc.	*crescendo*	(become louder)
dim.	*diminuendo*	(become softer)

Timbre

Timbre is best indicated in the full score, the music that the conductor of an ensemble would read. It is the responsibility of the conductor as interpreter not only to understand all of the instrumental and vocal parts but to actually hear in the mind's ear all the nuances of the music before it is performed. While each member of an ensemble is responsible for his or her separate part, it is the conductor who must interpret the total. Through appropriate gestures and indications, the conductor realizes as closely as possible what the composer desires.

THE CREATIVE PROCESS

In the twentieth century, two extremes are seen in the development of notation. George Crumb's music exemplifies one school of thought, with a very specific style of notation. Even while the resulting music has a free, improvised sound, the composer is controlling the performance as much as possible, with his deliberate notation (see Ex. 8.9).

In contrast, John Cage demonstrates another philosophy. He is less specific with the piano part of his Concert for Piano and Orchestra. This work, composed in 1957–58, leaves aspects of the performance to chance and to the performer. Motives are written on separate pieces of paper and chosen randomly by the performer. The notation is less specific than traditional twentieth-century notation, leaving room for interpretation by the performer (see Ex. 8.10).

Ex. 8.9

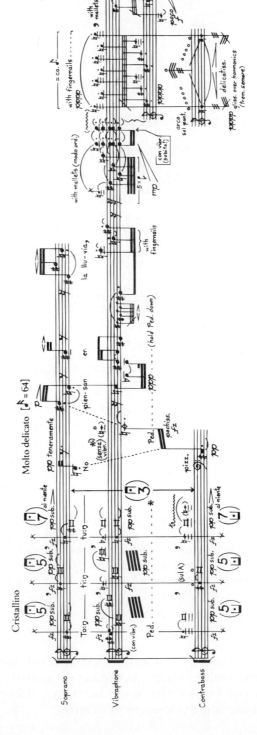

Crumb, *Madrigals Book One*. Copyright © 1971 by
C.F. Peters Corporation. Used by permission.

Ex. 8.10

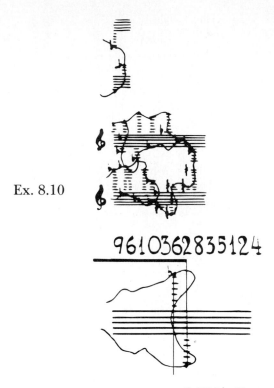

The requirements of the music often determine the form of notation. Bruno Bartolozzi, in developing new timbres for woodwind instruments, needed a new system of notation for these sounds (see Ex. 8.11).

Because of its unique qualities, Bartolozzi includes remarks on the interpretation of his notation:

> An unorthodox musical notation has been used, particularly as regards the duration and volume of sounds. The duration of sounds is indicated by the length of the horizontal line attached to the stem of each note, so that the "rhythm" of a phrase is derived from the proportions of the spaces between one note and another. Obviously, no meter is present. . . . The volume of sounds is shown by the thickness of the horizontal line. A thin line is pianissimo, a very thick one fortissimo.

—B. Bartolozzi
New Sounds for Woodwind

With Bartolozzi's system of notation a staff is still used to give specific indications of pitch, while duration is indicated spatially by the horizontal distance between pitches on the staff. Intensity differences are shown through the use of varying thicknesses of beams.

Ex. 8.11

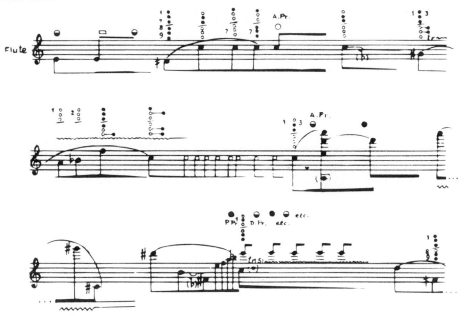

Bartolozzi, "Collage for Flute." © 1982 by Oxford
University Press. Used by permission of Oxford
University Press.

   While Bartolozzi and Crumb, through specific fingerings, careful timbre choice indications, and other composer-restricted regulations control
the performance to a high degree, other twentieth-century composers like
Cage have come full circle in their treatment of notation. Like early
Western versions, Cage and other contemporary composers give only general indications of pitch, duration, and intensity. The human element of
the musical equation, so long controlled by the composer, is being redis-
covered as a part of the performance process. Composers like Cage write
works or portions of works that are *aleatoric,* meaning left to chance. The
performer is given creative space—the forgetful monk's performance
would now be considered a creative part of the musical process.

JOURNAL ENTRY SUGGESTIONS

What weaknesses do you find in traditional music notation?

Our present system of notation in Western music has developed in very
specific ways. Develop your own system of notation that indicates in creative
and legible ways the elements of pitch, intensity, duration, and timbre.

Pitch Notation

In the previous chapter the general concepts of music notation were introduced. The present chapter expands this basic background material and introduces you to the specific system used in the notation of pitch.

PITCHES AND THE STAFF

As we discovered in Chapter 8 the graph of lines and spaces that is used for the notation of specific pitches is called a *staff*. We can use this staff to show the pitches of a melodic pattern we might wish to notate.

The melodic patterns used in the text tape have provided you with the beginnings of a melodic vocabulary. Through the use of traditional "solfège" syllables (on tape) you have been able to master some short melodies. You can now combine this ability with what you already know about notation to graphically represent these patterns. Using the staff and the treble clef we can graphically represent the pitches of the melodic pattern *do re mi fa sol.*

Ex. 9.1

do   re   mi   fa   sol

A note (o) is used to represent each pitch. In most cases the staff has enough lines and spaces to show the pitches. Sometimes, though, a pitch is lower than the bottom line of the staff or higher than the topmost line. When this happens, a short extension of the staff, called a *ledger line,* is used for the one pitch. In Example 9.1 *do* begins on the ledger line below the treble clef staff, and the note for *re* is positioned just above it. As we continue to move higher in pitch, notes are placed higher on the staff on succeeding lines and spaces. This provides us with a very specific position for each pitch. *Do* is positioned:

Ex. 9.2

while *sol* is found:

Ex. 9.3

The pattern *do mi sol* is notated:

Ex. 9.4

TONALITY

Most of the melodic examples we have worked with start or end on *do.* A special relationship between the pitches gives us a sense of "coming home" when we return to *do.* In musical terms, there is a feeling of *tonality,* with *do* as a *tonal center.* Many melodies found in music use this sense of tonality to create tension by pulling away from *do* and then resolving tension by coming home to *do.*

Ex. 9.5

We can give a clearer indication of duration with Bartolozzi-style duration extensions, using lines to extend the graphic representation of the note.

Ex. 9.9

This short melody begins on the tonal center, pulls away, then comes back home. We move from one pitch to the next nearest pitch, which creates conjunct motion. Other patterns we've used create a disjunct melody by skipping.

Ex. 9.7

The examples above are very short. Complete melodies are created by combining and varying this basic melodic vocabulary. Even with a limited vocabulary, tension can be created and resolved in many ways, and the natural phenomenon of tonality can be used to compose "workable" melodies. As you increase your melodic vocabulary and become more sensitive to the subtleties of melody, you will expand your possibilities for melodic development and for personal expression.

DIFFERENT TONAL CENTERS

One way of increasing melodic possibilities is to shift the tonal center and begin a melodic pattern on another pitch. We can maintain the relationships between pitches by beginning at a higher point, producing the sound of *do re mi fa sol sol fa mi re do*, but starting on a different pitch.

Ex. 9.8

We can begin other melodic patterns on this new pitch as well, maintaining the original relationship between pitches. The melodic pattern starts at a higher point:

Ex. 9.9

The above examples demonstrate that it is possible for *do*-to-*sol* patterns to occur in different places on the staff. This provides us with some creative flexibility, but it can also be somewhat confusing if we are trying to understand how to notate melodic patterns. We need a clearer way of showing *which do* is being used; which tonal center, and what specific pitches are notated. To avoid confusion, we need to be more specific in our method of naming pitches.

NAMING PITCHES IN TREBLE CLEF

You may recall that the original purpose of a clef was to provide a reference point on the staff. The treble clef (which we have been using for the examples in this chapter) shows where G is found.

Ex. 9.10

Pitches notated above this G will be higher, while those notated below G will be lower.

In music notation, the letters A, B, C, D, E, F, and G are used in the naming of pitches. As we move higher up the staff, we move forward through the alphabet. When we reach G we start again with another A and continue. Moving down the staff, we move backward through the alphabet. We now have the means for a more specific naming (and notation) of pitches. The pitches we have used so far in this chapter can now be given more specific names. We don't have to rely on *do* or *re*, and so on. Using the treble clef and staff, we can assign each pitch a letter name.

Ex. 9.11

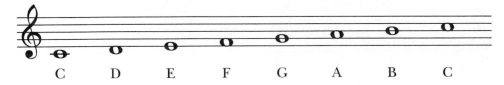

   C   D   E   F   G   A   B   C

The names of the pitches used for *do re mi fa sol* will therefore be different, depending on where on the staff the pitches are found. If C is the name of the pitch used as the tonal center, our pattern will begin with C as *do*. The pattern will be in the *key* of C.

Ex. 9.12

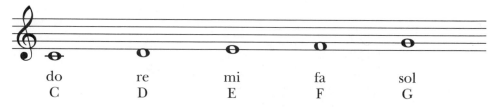

| do | re | mi | fa | sol |
| C | D | E | F | G |

We can sing *do re mi fa sol* with C as our tonal center, or with a tonal center of G; we can sing in the key of C or in the key of G. The pattern in the key of G starts on the pitch G.

Ex. 9.13

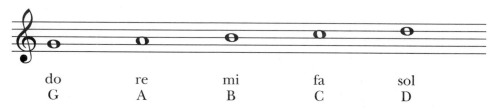

| do | re | mi | fa | sol |
| G | A | B | C | D |

NAMING PITCHES IN BASS CLEF

The bass clef, or F clef, can also be used to notate the same melodic patterns used in the G clef. The melodies would start on lower versions of C and G:

Ex. 9.14   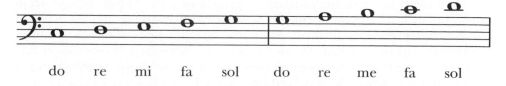   = F

Ex. 9.15

do re mi fa sol do re me fa sol

Our *do* to *sol* in the key of G extends beyond the staff, so that the pitches C and D require ledger lines. The ledger line used for C is the imaginary line shared by the treble clef staff and the bass clef staff;

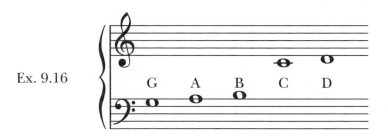 and 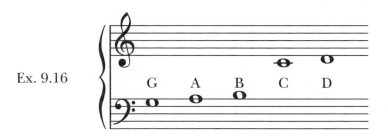 are the same pitch: C. We can use this ledger line as a midpoint between the two staves, and use the grand staff for the notation of pitches.

Ex. 9.16

SUMMARY

We have learned about the system of notation used in Western music to show specific pitches. Using the treble and bass clefs and their staves, we can notate some melodic patterns in the key of C and in the key of G. With our knowledge of pitch-specific notation, we can give a letter name to notes found in the grand staff.

Ex. 9.17

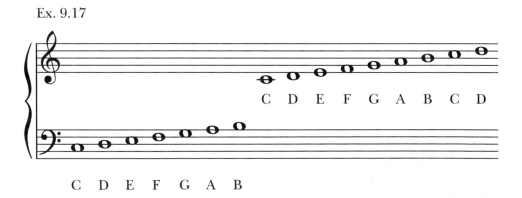

You need to learn to recognize each notated pitch quickly and accurately. Begin to drill note names in bass clef and in treble clef so that you become comfortable with the letter name of each line and each space in treble clef and in bass clef. Do not rely on the standard "Every Good Boy Does Fine" formula. That system does not promote music reading and is similar to multiplying 7 by 9 by adding $7 + 7 + 7 + 7 + 7 + 7 + 7 + 7 + 7$.

Learn to associate the lines and spaces of each staff with the names of the notes found there, and you will be moving toward mastering pitch notation.

WRITTEN ASSIGNMENT

A. The following are melodic patterns that have become familiar to you. They are notated in the key of C. Below each notated pitch, write the letter name of the note. Review the sound of each melodic pattern by singing each, using appropriate singing syllables. The first example is done for you.

1.

do   re   mi   do
C   D   E   C

2.

do   do   re   mi
___ ___ ___ ___

3.

do   re   mi   mi   fa   sol
___ ___ ___ ___ ___ ___

4.
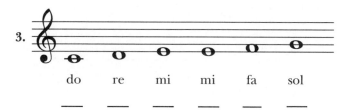

sol   fa   mi   re   mi   re   do
___   ___ ___ ___ ___ ___ ___

5.

___ ___ ___ ___ ___ ___

B. Below are some melodic patterns in the key of C. Notate these same melodies in the key of G, using a treble clef staff. In the new key, identify each notated pitch, writing in the name of the pitch below the note. The first is done for you.

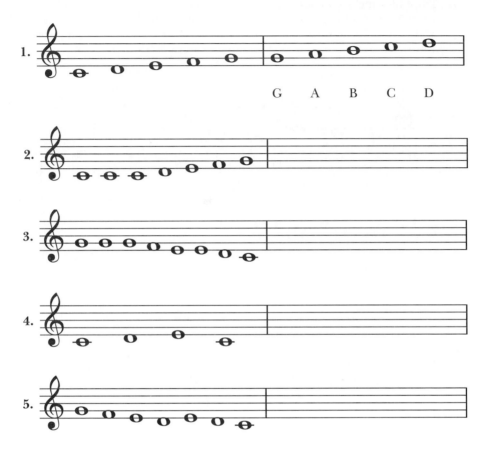

C. Notate the original patterns of section B (in the key of C) in bass clef. The first is done for you.

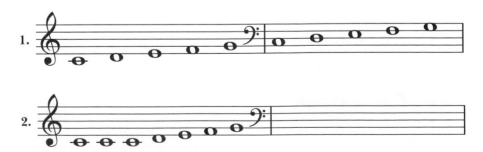

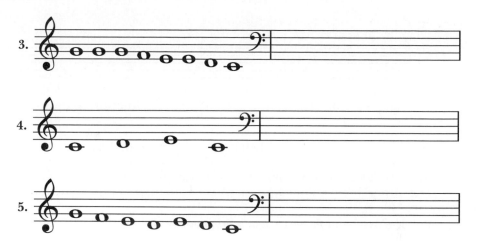

D. Copy your answers to section 2 in treble clef, then provide a bass clef notation of these same G major patterns.

1.

Original treble clef version (key of G)   Notation in bass clef

2.

Original treble clef version (key of G)   Notation in bass clef

3.

Original treble clef version (key of G)   Notation in bass clef

4.

Original treble clef version (key of G)   Notation in bass clef

5.

Original treble clef version (key of G)   Notation in bass clef

E. Answer each trivia question, then use the first letter of the answer to notate
the pitch with that letter name. For each example, use the clef indicated.
Give last names of proper names. Some examples may have multiple answers.
The first example is done for you. (Answers to trivia questions are found on
page 80.)

Ex. The first name of Superman's alter ego (bass clef): *Clark* Kent (notate a C)

Ex. 9.18

1. The last name of a famous composer who continued to write music even
after he became deaf (bass clef): _____

2. The *Minnow* left for a three-hour tour but was shipwrecked on this island
(treble clef): _____

3. The last name of the author of the science fiction "Foundation" series
(treble clef): _____

4. The number found on the black billiard ball (treble clef): _____

5. The name of the group in which Jim Morrison sang (bass clef): _____

6. The name of the second month of the year (bass clef): _____

7. The branch of science dealing with the study of life (treble clef): _____

8. The first name of the sixteenth president of the United States (treble clef): _____

9. The only two people in the baseball Hall of Fame who did not play baseball (both people) (bass clef): _____

10. The last name of the Indian leader who led people in a nonviolent revolt against British rule (bass clef): _____

CREATIVE ASSIGNMENT

Tape an original melody that uses patterns in the key of C. Use voice or instrument. Use the patterns found in this chapter, or similar ones, encompassing pitches found between *do* and *sol*. Begin on the tonic, gradually move away and create melodic tension, then come back home to the tonic note of C. Notate the pitches of your composition, using **o**s in the appropriate positions on a treble clef staff. Do not be concerned about specific rhythmic notation at this time, but give a general indication of duration through the use of Bartolozzi-style lines. These lines should be connected to notes to show an extended duration and can also be used to show changes in intensity, with thicker connecting lines indicating a louder pitch.

JOURNAL ENTRY SUGGESTIONS

A popular rock group is on trial for "obscenity" and "contributing to the delinquency of minors." You are serving as a jury member at this trial. How would you define *obscene*? Provide a transcript of the trial, as you would see it occur.

Write your own liner notes for an album made up of some of your favorite selections.

If you are familiar with the musical *The Sound of Music*, recall the song "Do, a Deer." Was this an effective way to teach young people how to sing? Why or why not? Based on your own singing experiences in this class, how realistic was the portrayal of the children's ease in mastering this material?

Answers to trivia questions   1. Beethoven   2. Gilligan's   3. Asimov   4. Eight 5. (The) Doors   6. February   7. Biology   8. Abe   9. Abbott and Costello 10. Gandhi

C H A P T E R   10

♪♪♪♪♪♪

Intervals and the Scale

INTERVALS

Chapter 2 discussed the concept of the doctrine of affections, the idea that a particular combination of sounds could be "sad," while another combination might excite "pleasant humors." This could theoretically be carried a step further. We could say that the distance from one pitch to the next pitch, just that small musical "idea," could have its own special character. The distance from one pitch to another is called an *interval,* and some people believe that different intervals have different properties. In a small way, we have used this difference in quality of intervals with some of our melodic patterns. Conjunct melodies have been created by moving from one pitch to the next nearest pitch—the distance of the interval from one pitch to the next has been small. In contrast, a melody that is disjunct has wider intervals. Some people hear conjunct melodies as smoother and more pleasant, and disjunct melodies as jagged and less restful. It could be that listeners respond to the intervalic relationships in melodies.

The Tritone

Just as the Greeks believed that certain melodies evoked specific emotional responses, certain intervals were held by the Catholic church of the Middle Ages to be "purer" than others. Indeed, one interval in music was said to be the least pure—the "interval of the devil," or *diabolus in musica* was the name given to the interval known as the tritone.

The *tritone* is an interval with a very specific sound. If you were to play a C and then play the pitch exactly halfway from that C to the next highest C, you would have created a tritone. You would think that a pitch found exactly halfway between two Cs would be just fine, but it does have an unstable sound to it—it is not a restful interval. Perhaps because of this, the church outlawed the tritone and did not permit music in church services to utilize this interval. For centuries, this interval was not heard or was treated very carefully as a dissonance and never used as the basic melodic element of a composition.

Leonard Bernstein uses the tritone as the main motive in "Maria," from *West Side Story*. The unstable quality of this interval is exploited by Bernstein to portray the poignancy of the moment and to provide a strong sense of momentum to the piece. After the contemplative opening section, an ascending figure is used for the word *Maria* and begins with a tritone, which then resolves upward. This initial motive is used throughout the piece. Sequential variations and changes of intervals are used in conjunction with rhythmic motives. Various orchestral combinations provide changes in timbre and intensity, but the original tritone motive remains the characteristic element of the work.

Paul Winter is a performer and composer who has been attracted to the new and unusual in music. He has used bird calls, whale songs (see Chapter 1 Listening Example), and wolf howls as basic material for his compositions. When he was asked by the dean of the Cathedral of St. John the Divine in New York City to write a Mass, he turned to the sounds of nature for source material.

During the course of time, the Mass has become more than a spiritual celebration. When writing music for a Mass, composers have worked with the text and elements of this form to create personal, individual compositions. Such compositions stand on their own outside the celebration of the Mass proper. Winter has continued this tradition in his *Missa Gaia*.

As Winter became involved in the project, the theme of a Mass to celebrate God and all of God's creation began to emerge. His *Missa Gaia*, or *Earth Mass*, became an expression of a desire for harmonious existence and a respect for all life. The Kyrie section of the *Earth Mass* seems to exemplify this basic idea, as it attempts to dispel centuries-old myth and doctrine.

The Kyrie is given this name because of the Latin text used at that point in the Mass:

Kyrie eleison   (Lord have mercy)
Christe eleison   (Christ have mercy)
Kyrie eleison   (Lord have mercy)

This section of the Mass has a built-in ternary form that many composers have used when writing music for the Mass. The Kyrie has a short text that can be repeated to develop continuity in a composition. Winter works with these elements but adds an individual stamp to his Kyrie.

A prerecorded wolf howl is used as basic melodic material for the Kyrie. The wolf is heard at the very beginning of the piece, introducing the melodic material that will form the basis for the entire composition. The very first notes of the howl present the "forbidden" interval of the tritone. Presented in this setting, Winter seems to be calling for the abolishment of the old ideas, asking for a new freedom in music and in the treatment of life on earth. The Greek Gaia concept holds that the earth is a living thing and that we are all interconnected. Our treatment of another life form affects us. Just as the wolf has been an outcast in society, the tritone has been labeled "evil" in some musical circles. Winter asks us to set aside these prejudices and permit the wolf to coexist with us; to allow the wolf's "song," in all its power and strangeness, to be heard in the setting of a Mass.

Throughout the Kyrie, the tritone is heard as a celebration of life; indeed, the middle section of the Kyrie uses some very primitive-sounding percussion instruments to help us develop that feeling of celebration.

    Winter, Kyrie, from *Missa Gaia*

With the Kyrie, we hear the tritone used as the foundation for a complete composition.

Other Intervals

The tritone is one specific interval. This interval, however, is not as common as some others. A number of common intervals are produced when moving from one pitch to another. If we use a C as a starting point each time, we can give a general name to intervals formed as we move up from that pitch. If we move from C to the next nearest note, D, we will have moved the interval of a 2nd; if we move from C to E, we will have moved a 3rd. In each case, to name the interval, we simply count the C as 1 and count through each line and space to our next notated pitch. All of the intervals from C to the next C are named here:

Ex. 10.1

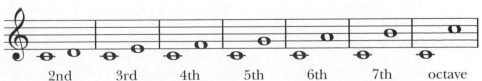

     2nd   3rd   4th   5th   6th   7th   octave

This provides us with the general names of intervals. We could begin with any pitch, use it as a starting point, and create the intervals of a 2nd, a 3rd, a 4th, a 5th, a 6th, a 7th, and an octave:

Ex. 10.2

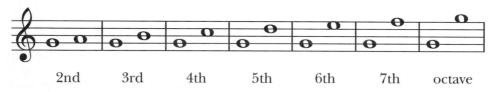

2nd   3rd   4th   5th   6th   7th   octave

As with pitch names, we can be more specific when we name intervals. The tritone has its special sound because of the specific intervalic relationship that is formed. Some 2nds are smaller than others; the same is true of 3rds, 4ths, and so on.

The distance from one letter name to the next nearest letter (moving conjunctly) is the interval of a *major 2nd* each time, with two exceptions. E to F and B to C are both smaller in distance than a major 2nd. In both of these cases, the interval involved is a *minor 2nd*. To put it another way, the sound of *do* to *re* is a major 2nd, while the sound of *ti* to *do* is a minor 2nd.

The minor 2nd is the smallest interval we use in Western music, although the music of other cultures use smaller intervals. Major seconds and minor seconds form the basis of the melodic patterns we have been working with.

If we move from one letter name to the next, covering all of the letter names from one C to the next C, we will have a pattern of major 2nds and minor 2nds that has a particular sound. Moving this way provides a series of pitches that make up a *major scale*.

Ex. 10.3

maj. 2nd maj. 2nd min. 2nd   maj. 2nd maj. 2nd maj. 2nd min. 2nd

The sound of a major scale results when we produce this specific series of major and minor 2nds within the space of an octave. We have already discovered that *do* to *re* has the sound of a major 2nd. A major 2nd is also found between *re* and *mi*. The next interval of the major scale is a minor 2nd, from *mi* to *fa*. Major 2nds occur between other pitches, except for the final interval of *ti* to *do*, where we find the last minor 2nd. This pattern of major and minor 2nds helps create the sense of tonality we learned about earlier, especially if we are moving up toward the octave tonic. The final minor 2nd helps pull us home to *do*. We can indicate the position of minor 2nds in a major scale with a caret symbol (ʌ):

Ex. 10.4

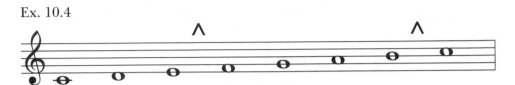

As we will see in later chapters, a major scale can be created with any pitch as a starting point. We need to make adjustments to maintain the correct relationship of major and minor 2nds, but as long as the series of major and minor 2nds follows the same pattern, we will have the sound of a major scale.

THE CREATIVE PROCESS

Though good melodies seldom use a complete major scale in its original form, the major scale often serves as basic material for melodies. Some of the intervalic relationships that are created within a major scale are used to provide motion, tension, and repose, to move away from the tonic and gradually return. Melodic contours (as seen in Chapter 5) can be created with the major scale as basic material. The contours created can be simple, as are the descending and ascending lines of "Joy to the World."

Ex. 10.5

"Joy to the World" uses a descending major scale in the first phrase; melodies do not often use such obvious scale patterns. This Christmas carol also uses sequential and exact repetition and balances this repetition with melodic variety between the two phrases.

"Irish Tune from County Derry" has a greater variety of intervals. Where "Joy to the World" uses conjunct motion except for one interval of a 5th, "Irish Tune" uses 3rds and 4ths in a number of places. These disjunct intervals are combined with conjunct motion and provide variety. The melody, in the key of F, does not begin on the tonic. Example 10-6, the first phrase of the tune, also does not end on the tonic. The variety of intervals and melodic motion and the more complex wave contour work with the tension of avoiding the tonic to provide variety and interest in a short span of time.

Ex. 10.6

WRITTEN ASSIGNMENT

A. Give the general name of each interval (2nd, 5th, etc.).

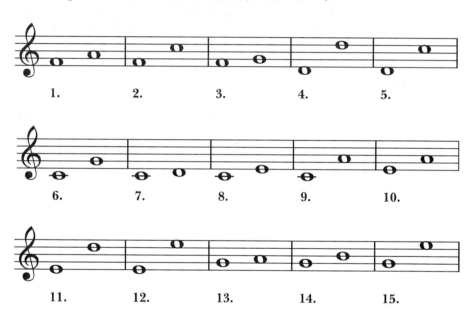

B. Write the proper note above the given pitch to complete each interval.

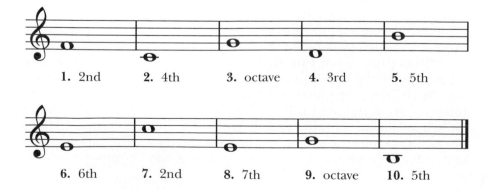

1. 2nd   2. 4th   3. octave   4. 3rd   5. 5th

6. 6th   7. 2nd   8. 7th   9. octave   10. 5th

C. Identify each interval as a major 2nd or a minor 2nd.

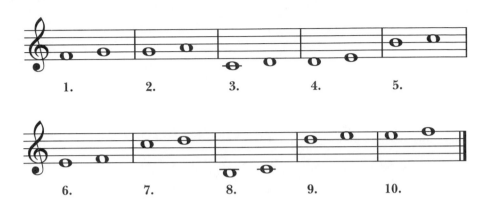

CREATIVE ASSIGNMENT

Use the complete C major scale as source material for an original melody for voice or for traditional or nontraditional instrument. Begin on the C below the staff in treble clef and find creative ways to pull away from the tonic, create tension, and gradually climb to the octave C as a cadence point. Use rhythms you have learned so far (again, with no concern for notation) to create motion and rest in your short melody. Be aware of major and minor 2nds and their function in the development of a sense of tonality in your composition. Save your melody on tape and give a general indication of duration with Bartolozzi-style notation. Give specific indications for intensity changes, using traditional Italian terms and abbreviations (*p*, *mf*, etc.), and graphic symbols.

JOURNAL ENTRY SUGGESTIONS

Plato thought that certain melodies could alter the feelings and thinking of the young people of Greek society. Though we are not as sensitive to the possibility that a certain pitch or melodic pattern can have power over listeners in the same way, some people today seem to hold similar views about certain forms of rock music. Comment.

♪♪♪♪♪♪

Pitch and the Keyboard

You have been introduced to scales and melodic patterns by hearing them first. It can be more helpful to use a keyboard so that you can hear *and see* the difference in intervals and scale patterns. Associating each pitch with its location on a keyboard can be helpful.

The C located on the ledger line below the treble staff can also be notated in the bass staff on the ledger line above the staff. This C is in the middle of the grand staff and is usually found in the middle of a keyboard as well. C has a specific location on the staff, and a specific location on the keyboard.

Ex. 11.1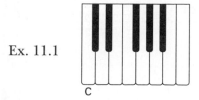

With keyboard location of pitches, all Cs are located in the same relative position: *to the left of the grouping of two black keys.* Each time the white key to the left of this grouping of two black keys is depressed, a C results. The farther to the right on the keyboard, the higher the C—different octaves are produced.

Different types of keyboards have varying numbers of Cs. Shorter keyboards have fewer octaves, while full-sized keyboards provide a greater number of Cs. In any event, a C can always be found in the same relative location.

Some other patterns that we have notated can be located on a keyboard diagram:

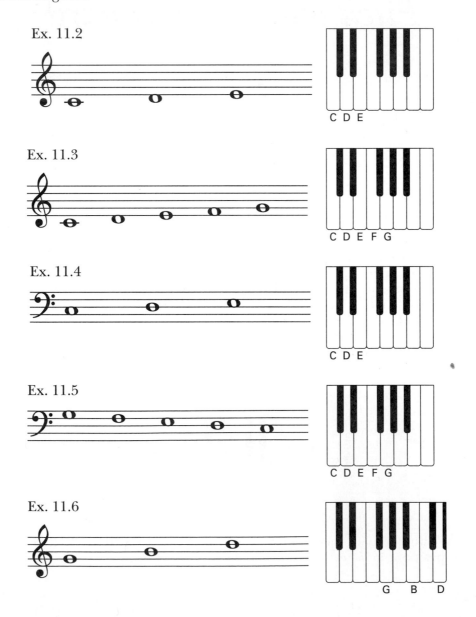

Ex. 11.2

C D E

Ex. 11.3

C D E F G

Ex. 11.4

C D E

Ex. 11.5

C D E F G

Ex. 11.6

G   B   D

Examples 11.2 to 11.6 show a connection between notated pitches and their relative location on a keyboard. These examples can also give a graphic representation of specific intervals. We can see the distance of a minor 2nd, and the larger interval of a 3rd. The keyboard can help us remember and identify intervals and melodic patterns.

At the end of Chapter 10 we created a complete C major scale by starting on C and continuing up the staff to the next octave C. When we did this, we created the interval of a minor 2nd between the third and fourth notes and between the seventh and eighth notes of the scale; all other intervals were major 2nds. A major scale can be built beginning on any pitch, as long as this specific arrangement of major 2nds and minor 2nds is maintained.

The C major scale uses letter names from C to C. If we were to sit down at a keyboard to play this scale, we would use the white keys of the keyboard, starting with C

Ex. 11.7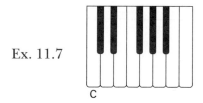

and continuing to the right (moving "up" the scale) to the next C on the keyboard:

Ex. 11.8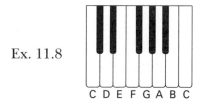

You can see that when we play the C major scale at a keyboard, there is a black key between each note of the scale except where we have minor 2nds. A minor 2nd is the smallest interval in Western music; we see that with the keyboard—when we move a minor 2nd, we move from one key on the keyboard to the next adjacent key. In the case of the C major scale, we move from one white key to another white key on the keyboard, with no black keys between. With a C major scale, the minor 2nd from E to F is played by moving from one white key to another white key. The same is true for the interval B to C. In all other cases, a black key falls between the notes of the major scale. The interval of a major 2nd equals *two* half steps. On a keyboard, we need to move up (to the right) *two* keys.

The black keys on the keyboard became important when we want to form a major scale that begins on a note other than C. To maintain the same arrangement of minor 2nds and major 2nds, we need to make some adjustments to the pitch names; we need to use some of the black keys to do this. Chapter 12 will look at some of these scales.

WRITTEN ASSIGNMENT

A. Write the letter name of each pitch in the proper location on the keyboard diagram provided. The first is done for you.

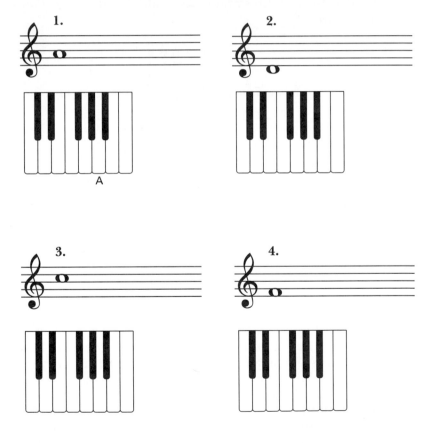

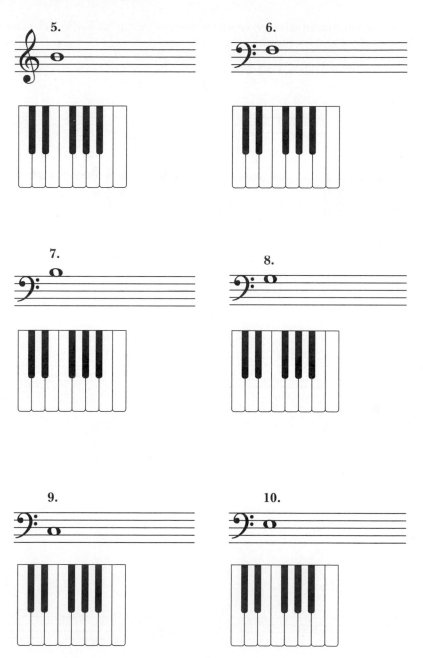

B. Provide the name of each note of the following melodic patterns in the proper keyboard location.

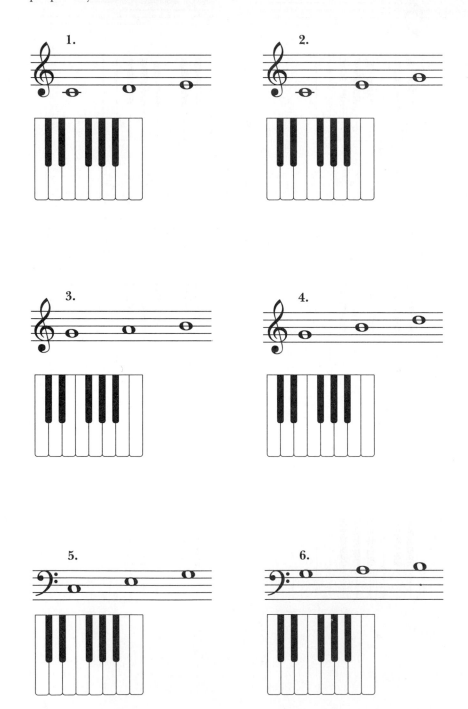

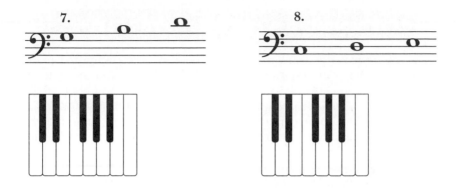

PERFORMANCE ASSIGNMENT

Practice singing each example, then play each at the keyboard.

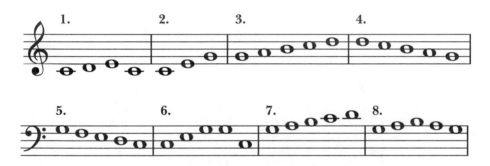

LISTENING ASSIGNMENT

Try to identify the tonal centers of some of the music you hear. Use a keyboard to give a specific pitch name to the key you identify, or simply listen for *do* in the music you hear.

CREATIVE ASSIGNMENT

Choose either a C major tonality or a G major tonality. Select two to four pitches as source material for a keyboard composition. Your assignment must be limited to your chosen pitches (in any octave), but you may combine them in a polyphonic or homophonic texture, if you choose. Explore the melodic tendencies of the specific pitches you have chosen and strive for a balance of repetition and variety (including form). Use cadences that give clear indications of sections. Do not notate your assignment, but save your final result on your Creative-Assignment tape.

JOURNAL ENTRY SUGGESTIONS

What differences can you see and hear between the traditional piano and some of today's contemporary keyboards? Are there differences in styles of playing?

Is it possible for different people to produce different timbres on a piano? If so, how? What are some experimental ways of playing the piano that you can think of that might produce completely different sounds on that instrument?

Other Scales

THE G MAJOR SCALE

To create a complete major scale beginning on G, we must use the correct arrangement of major and minor 2nds. Minor 2nds must appear between the third and fourth notes, and between the seventh and eighth notes; major 2nds are found between all other pitches. First, we'll position notes on the staff, in ascending order, from G to G:

Ex. 12.1

We can also locate these pitches on a keyboard diagram:

Ex. 12.2

G A B C D E F G

We already know that there is a minor 2nd between B and C—we saw that in our C major scale. Fortunately, this works to our advantage with the G major scale. We need a minor 2nd between the third and fourth notes of our major scale, and B to C is a minor 2nd.

Ex. 12.3

We can use what we know about major scales to check the other intervals of our present G scale. For the rest of the scale we know that we need major 2nds between all notes except the seventh and eighth, where we need another minor 2nd.

Ex. 12.4

E to F is a minor 2nd, and our G major scale needs a *major* 2nd at this point in the scale. We need to increase the distance between these two pitches by raising the F. We must use a sharp (♯) to raise the pitch.

Ex. 12.5

A sharp is placed directly to the left of the pitch to be altered, on the same line or in the same space as the pitch. With an F♯ (F-sharp) now in place, we have the correct arrangement of major and minor 2nds—we have the sound of a major scale.

Ex. 12.6

We can check the arrangement of major and minor 2nds against our keyboard diagram:

Ex. 12.7

Where we need a minor 2nd, we move from one key to the next adjacent key; major 2nds involve skipping a key. In the case of the G major scale, an F♯ is played on the black key just to the left of G. With the F♯ in place, the correct arrangement of major and minor 2nds is maintained. Other major scales will require sharps as well.

THE D MAJOR SCALE

The D major scale is another scale that requires some adjustment to the natural notes to maintain the proper arrangement of major and minor 2nds. As with other scales, we begin our D major scale by first placing notes on the staff in ascending order, from D to D:

Ex. 12.8

We are using carets to indicate where minor 2nds are needed in our scale; all other intervals will be major 2nds. To have the minor 2nds where required in the D major scale, we must make some adjustments to the present arrangement. E to F is not a major 2nd, but a minor 2nd. We must increase the distance between these pitches, just as we did with the G major scale, by using a sharp to raise the F to F♯. This gives us the necessary major 2nd interval between E and F♯. Do we need to make any further adjustments? As we continue up the scale, we have F♯ to G, which is a minor 2nd (we have solved two problems at once when we raised the F to F♯). G to A is a major 2nd, as is A to B. Our next problem occurs with B to C. We know that this interval is a minor 2nd, not a major 2nd (remember our C major scale, and the G major scale?). We must change the C to C♯ to adjust the interval to a major 2nd.

Ex. 12.9

If all is right, the last interval of our major scale should be a minor 2nd. C♯ to D *is* a minor 2nd, so our D major scale is now correct. We can check the scale against our keyboard diagram:

Ex. 12.10

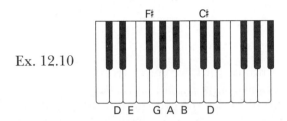

So far, we have used the sharp to raise pitches to maintain the proper arrangement of major and minor 2nds in the creation of new major scales. The sharp is just one *accidental* that is used to change a pitch. There will also be cases where we need to *lower* a pitch. The accidental used for this purpose is the *flat* (♭).

THE F MAJOR SCALE

The F major scale is one that requires the use of a flat. If we position notes on the staff, using carets to mark the locations of minor 2nds, we will see where adjustments must be made:

Ex. 12.11

With our keyboard diagram we can clearly see that the minor second we need between the third and fourth notes is not present:

Ex. 12.12

Our problem occurs between A and B. At this point in our major scale, we need a minor 2nd, not the major 2nd that is present. We do not want to change the A, however, because that would change the intervals that are already correct. We need to adjust the B by lowering it to a B♭:

Ex. 12.13

Its location on the keyboard:

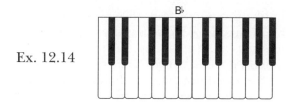

Ex. 12.14

We now have the required minor 2nd between the third and fourth notes. No other adjustments are necessary—major and minor 2nds are found in their proper places.

Ex. 12.15

THE B♭ MAJOR SCALE

Other major scales require flats. In all cases (except with the F major scale), these scales will contain a flat within the name of the scale itself. The B♭ major scale is one of these scales.

Ex. 12.16

To maintain the proper arrangement of major and minor 2nds, a flat has been used to lower the E to E♭. If we check the scale against the keyboard diagram, we see the proper progression of major and minor 2nds:

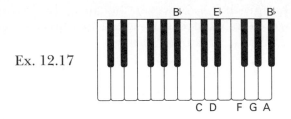

Ex. 12.17

THE CHROMATIC SCALE

We have been using sharps to raise pitches and flats to lower them. The distance from B to B♭, like a minor 2nd, is the smallest interval possible in Western music; unlike the minor 2nd, though, which moves from one letter name to another letter name, B to B♭ uses the *same* letter name. This distance is a less specific interval called a *half step*. Anytime we move from one pitch to the next nearest pitch we are moving a half step, but we may not have a minor 2nd. C to C♯ is a half step but not a minor 2nd. C to D♭, the same half step, can also be called a minor 2nd—this interval moves from one letter name to another. C♯ and D♭ are two different names for the same pitch. Two notes of the same pitch that are given different names are said to be *enharmonic*.

We can see half steps at work in the chromatic scale. The *chromatic scale* is a series of half steps within an octave. The "automatic" half steps found between E and F and between B and C require no flat or sharp. In all other cases, we use sharps to raise each pitch a half step as we move higher up the chromatic scale and flats to lower pitches on the way down. Thus, when creating (musicians say "spelling") a chromatic scale, we use enharmonic spellings. In place of the ascending F♯, a G♭ is used while descending. These enharmonic equivalents can be found throughout the chromatic scale and provide most of the sharped and flatted notes that are used in creating other major scales.

Ex. 12.18

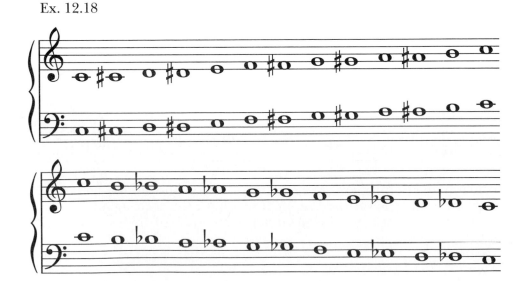

Containing all of the half steps within an octave, the chromatic scale can serve as a reference for the spelling of most major scales. For example, using the chromatic scale we can check the notes of a D major scale. Beginning on the D, we can see where minor 2nds and major 2nds will fall. A major 2nd up from D will bring us through D♯ to E; another major 2nd brings us past F to F♯. We can continue through the chromatic scale, using the appropriate pitches to spell a D major scale.

We can use the descending form of the chromatic scale, with its flats, to check major scales that use those accidentals. An F major scale can be found within the chromatic scale, as we work out the major and minor 2nds needed for that major scale.

THE CREATIVE PROCESS

During the early history of Western music, just a few tonal centers were used in the creation of music. Part of the reason for this concerned the limitations of the instruments themselves. Eventually the technology of instrument making developed to the point where more pitches were available to the performer. As composers and performers strived to create new and more exciting sounds, different keys were explored, and the vocabulary of music making increased.

Today, we can choose from a variety of tonal centers. We might find, like the Greeks, that different melodic patterns and different tonal centers affect us in different ways. We might consider the key of G more uplifting than that of C or feel that the key of D is better suited to lively dance music. With a greater choice of keys and an ever-expanding palette of melodic patterns, our creative possibilities are limited only by our imagination.

SUMMARY

We have created major scales in the keys of C, G, D, F, and B♭. In creating these new major scales we applied the arrangement of major 2nds and minor 2nds required for a major scale to a new tonal center. Using accidentals, we made adjustments to pitches to fit this pattern of major and minor 2nds.

By following this same procedure, we can create other major scales. As a double-check, we can also use the chromatic scale as a resource when choosing the proper pitches in a new key.

WRITTEN ASSIGNMENT

A. Raise each notated pitch a half step by placing a sharp directly to the left of the note, in the same space or on the same line.

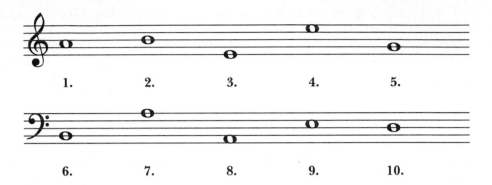

B. Lower each notated pitch through the use of a flat.

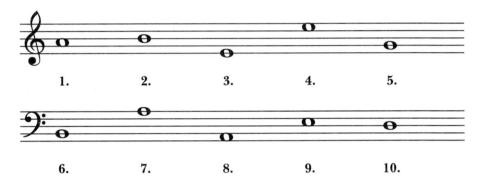

C. Use the treble staff to notate each example. Remember that we *read* C♯ but notate that pitch with the sharp *to the left* of the note.

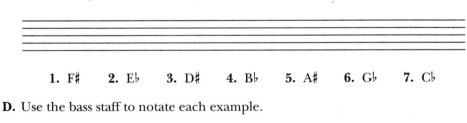

    1. F♯   **2.** E♭   **3.** D♯   **4.** B♭   **5.** A♯   **6.** G♭   **7.** C♭

D. Use the bass staff to notate each example.

    1. A♭   **2.** G♯   **3.** D♭   **4.** C♯   **5.** B♭   **6.** E♭   **7.** F♭

E. Spell a chromatic scale beginning on the pitch given. Place **o**s on the staff, and use sharps ascending and flats descending. Remember where the automatic half steps are found!

F. Spell the following major scales, placing **o**s on the staff provided, using the clef of your choice. Use sharps or flats as needed, and remember to place accidentals directly to the left of the pitch to be altered, on the same line or in the same space as the pitch. Use the chromatic scale on page 105 to check the arrangement of major and minor 2nds. Remember to move from one letter name to the next letter name. Use carets to indicate placement of minor 2nds.

1. A major

2. E major

3. E♭ major

4. A♭ major

CREATIVE ASSIGNMENT

Create a two-phrase period that uses the entire range of either a C major scale or a G major scale. End the first phrase on *re* or *sol*, and end the second phrase on *do*. Be aware of your use of repeated melodic and rhythmic ideas and consciously utilize one of the melodic contours we have studied. Perform your composition using voice, piano, or another instrument, and save it on your Creative-Assignment tape.

JOURNAL ENTRY SUGGESTIONS

Why do we have different major scales in music? What are the benefits of having a variety of tonal centers?

If you are familiar with music of another culture, comment on the use of scales in this music. How is the sound of the music different?

Key Signatures

MAJOR KEYS THROUGH TWO SHARPS AND TWO FLATS

We have created major scales in the keys of C, G, D, F, and B♭. We can now work in these keys by using the notes found in the major scale. If we want to compose or perform music in the key of G, we need to use an F♯ rather than an F to provide the tonal center of G. F♯s will be used throughout a piece of music in the key of G, while B♭s will be used in the key of F. Once an accidental is used in a measure, it is in effect for the rest of the measure. This avoids to some degree the unnecessary replication of a sharp or flat, but the process of indicating individual accidentals can still be tedious.

Because all major scales except C require the repeated use of one or more accidentals, a shortcut is taken to indicate the accidentals needed: the key signature.

A *key signature* is the arrangement of sharps or flats found at the beginning of a piece of music and on every line thereafter, indicating the tonal center of the music. If a piece is in the key of G, a sharp is placed at the beginning of every line of the music, just after the clef. The sharp is placed on the top line of the treble staff and on the F line of the bass staff.

Ex. 13.1

The key of D, which uses an F♯ and a C♯, indicates these two sharps. The key signature for the key of D is

Ex. 13.2

Major keys with flats indicate the flats in a similar manner:

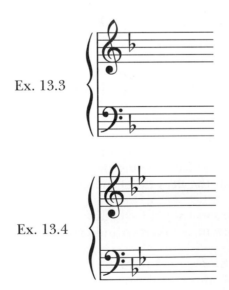

Ex. 13.3

Ex. 13.4

Key signatures are used to give an immediate indication of the tonal center of a piece and to avoid the repeated use of accidentals. While the use of key signatures overcomes the need for repetitive accidentals, the practice places a burden on the performer, who must remember to use throughout the entire piece the accidental or accidentals indicated.

Here are some examples of key signatures at work:

Ex. 13.5

Ex.13.6

Ex.13.7

The key signature at the beginning of each of the above examples provides us with important information about its tonal center. Even though Exs. 13.5 and 13.6 do not begin on the tonic, the key signature helps us identify the key of the piece. The key signature of Ex. 13.5 indicates that the selection is in the key of D. F♯, the third note of the D major scale, is the starting pitch; the melody begins on *mi*. The next example, written in the bass staff, is the same melody written in another key, the key of F. The melody begins on *mi*, which is an A in our new key of F. Example 13.7 is a notation of the second phrase, which comes to a close on the tonic.

Finally, we see what should be a familiar melody, presented in the key of G:

Ex.13.8

OTHER KEY SIGNATURES

So far, we have dealt with the keys of C, G, D, A, E, F, B♭, E♭, and A♭. The key signature for the key of C has no sharps and flats; the treble staff key signatures for the other keys are given here:

Ex. 13.9

The same key signatures can be found in the bass staff:

Ex. 13.10

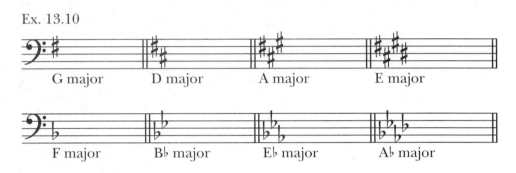

THE CREATIVE PROCESS

The careful notation of a musical composition is an important aspect of the creative process, helping the performer re-create the original intent of the composer. As you discover more about the practice of music notation, you will become more adept yourself at deciphering written music and more accurate in notating your own creative efforts. You will be able to provide a performer other than yourself with the tools needed to properly interpret your intentions. The notated version of your composition will come to look like the following example:

Ex. 13.11

This example is the beginning of a melody. Allegro maestoso gives an indication of the tempo and character of the piece. The key signature shows the tonality, and specific pitches are notated on the treble staff. Dynamic levels and changes in intensity are shown. In addition to these familiar markings there are also some notational devices for meter and rhythm that need to be explored further in Chapter 14.

WRITTEN ASSIGNMENT

A. Determine the key of each example. On the staff provided, notate the major scale of that major key, *without* the use of a key signature. Use appropriate accidentals.

B. The following melodies are presented without the aid of key signatures.
Determine the major key of each example based on the melodic patterns
and accidentals used. All of the necessary accidentals for a particular key may
not be found in some examples; you will need to do some visual and aural
work to determine keys. Remember, too, that an accidental holds true for
the entire measure.

On the staff provided, rewrite each example, using the appropriate key signature. The first is done for you.

When you have completed the examples, practice singing each, using appropriate syllables. You should then be able to identify the name of each
melody.

CREATIVE ASSIGNMENT

Work at the keyboard, with another instrument, or with your voice, and experiment with the new tonality of A major until you feel comfortable working in this key. Create an original melody in the key of A. Your melody should have an A–B structure and should be composed of two phrases per section. Submit two notated versions to accompany the tape of your melody, one that does not use a key signature, and a second that does. Your notation should indicate each specific pitch of your creative assignment and should give a general indication of duration.

If specific changes in intensity become an important part of your creative assignment, use them, and give an indication of these changes in your notation.

JOURNAL ENTRY SUGGESTIONS

What are the benefits of key signatures? What might be some drawbacks?

Read a *New York Times* music review. Clip it and save it in your journal. Analyze the review, searching for subject areas of concern to the reviewer. How does the reviewer go about commenting on the piece (or concert)? Are comments broad and general, or in specific areas? What is good and bad about the review process? How do reviewer comments compare with the process you are often asked to follow when critiquing music for this class?

Write your own review for the *New York Times,* as you think it should be written. Choose a selection you like very much, or perhaps one you dislike a great deal.

Rhythmic Notation

RHYTHMIC VOCABULARY IN DUPLE METER

As with melodic notation, we can use previously mastered rhythmic pat-terns to learn rhythmic notation. The basic *du* will be represented by ♩ while *du de* will be notated ♫ . We can notate the learned rhythmic pat-tern of *du du du du* as:

Ex. 14.1

The ♩ (*du*) is our unit of rhythmic value, receiving one beat. We are using pat-terns in a duple meter, so beats are grouped in twos. The $\frac{2}{4}$ at the beginning of the pattern indicates a duple meter. *Barlines* (|) are used to indicate the end of a measure of two beats, and a *double bar* (‖) indicates the end of a section.

Rhythms in a duple meter have patterns that take up two beats per mea-sure. The abbreviations "S" and "W" indicate strong and weak beats in the measure (we will see these indications in other chapter examples). Various combinations of rhythms are possible; some familiar ones are given here. Practice these examples, keeping a steady beat and using rhythm syllables.

Ex. 14.2

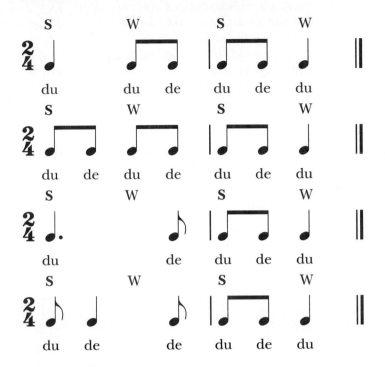

Other rhythmic patterns with which we have worked include

Ex. 14.3

As with melodic notation, rhythmic notation can be very specific. A "hierarchy" of note values exists in rhythmic notation. The ♩ is called a *quarter note.* The amount of time it takes to perform two quarter notes equals one *half note,* which is notated ♩ .

This entire system of rhythmic notation begins with the *whole note,* 𝅝, which is equal to four quarter notes, and therefore receives four beats. A whole note could not be used in a meter of two because there would not be enough "room" in a measure for four beats, but a meter with four beats per measure can accommodate this note.

We can outline the "hierarchy" of rhythmic values as follows:

Ex. 14.4

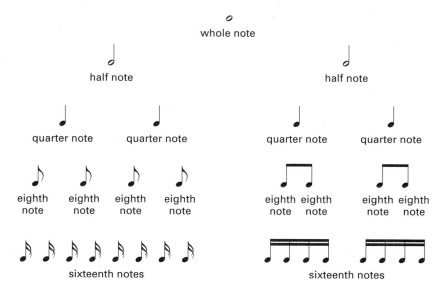

Eighth notes and sixteenth notes are usually beamed together. As shown above, we see single eighth and sixteenth notes, with a *notehead, stem,* and *flag* for each note (sixteenth notes require a double flag). When two or more eighth notes or sixteenth notes are grouped together, a *beam* replaces the flag (a double beam for the double flag of the sixteenth notes). We see these beams used in the right-hand column of the above example.

The *meter signature* of $\frac{2}{4}$ tells us not only that there are two beats in a measure, but that a quarter note receives one of those beats. If a piece has four beats per measure and the quarter note is still the unit of measure (receiving one beat), then the meter signature $\frac{4}{4}$ is used. Likewise, music that uses another note value as its unit of measure indicates this in the lower number of the meter signature. $\frac{4}{8}$ indicates music with four beats in a measure, with the eighth note receiving one beat.

COMPOUND DUPLE METER

So far, we have been dealing with *simple duple meter*. With such a meter, each of the two beats in a measure is divided evenly into two (the *du* is divided into *du de*). Subdivisions like *du ta de ta* involve a further breaking down of the beat by *twos*. *Compound meters*, however, divide the beat into *threes*.

The *du da di* patterns you have mastered are in a *compound meter*. Once again, the *du* is the unit of measure, but we now have a grouping of three for every beat.

Ex. 14.5

As you can see from this example, the rhythmic unit of measure (the note value that receives one beat) is now a *dotted* quarter note. Because our hierarchy of note values is based on divisions of two (two eighth notes equal a quarter note, etc.), when we have a compound meter, we must use the dot beside a quarter note to show that there are *three* eighth notes in that unit of measure. A dot beside a note indicates that we should increase the rhythmic value of the note again by half. A dotted whole note equals a whole note plus half of that; a dotted half note equals a half note plus half of that (a half note plus a quarter note). Our dotted quarter note equals a quarter note plus one half of that (a quarter note plus an eighth note, or three eighth notes).

In a compound meter, then, the unit of measure is a dotted note, and we group divisions of the beat into threes. In the example above, the *du* equals a dotted quarter note, and *du da di* is notated as three eighth notes beamed together. Other ⁶⁄₈ patterns include

Ex. 14.6

Where $\frac{2}{4}$ indicated the number of beats per measure as well as the of measure, $\frac{6}{8}$ does not seem to do the same. Music in $\frac{6}{8}$ has *two* beats per measure, not six (it is a duple meter), with a division of each beat into threes. A $\frac{6}{8}$ meter signature would seem to indicate six beats per measure, with the *eighth note* receiving a beat. At a very slow tempo (e.g., adagio) this would be the case, but with moderate and quick tempos, we feel two beats per measure. You will need to translate compound meter signatures to discover the true unit of measure.

Because the unit of measure in compound meters is divided into threes instead of twos, the *division* of the beat is shown in the meter signature. $\frac{6}{8}$ shows the eighth note as the division of the beat; six eighth notes are found in each measure. We know that $\frac{6}{8}$ is a compound meter that groups eighth notes in threes, so we can divide the six by three to arrive at the true number of beats per measure. Likewise, if we group three eighth notes together, we have a dotted quarter note—this is the true unit of measure in $\frac{6}{8}$ time.

With any compound meter, start with the note value indicated by the bottom number of the meter signature, then move up (toward the whole note) in the note value hierarchy. Dot the note you come to, and you will have the note that receives one beat in each measure. Follow this procedure for any compound meter signature. The trick, of course, is in discovering whether or not the meter is compound.

> *Any meter signature whose top number is a multiple of three (excluding three itself) is a compound meter. Treat it as such, and determine the true unit of measure accordingly.*

With this rule in mind, we can identify a meter signature as compound or simple, and determine the unit of measure.

$\frac{15}{16}$ has a top number that is evenly divisible by three; fifteen divided by three equals five, so that is the number of beats in each measure. If we group three sixteenth notes together, we have a dotted eighth (from the sixteenth, go up the hierarchy of note values to an eighth and dot the note).

$\frac{8}{8}$ has a top number that is *not* evenly divisible by three, so we must treat this meter signature as a simple meter and read it as is: eight beats per measure, with the eighth note receiving one beat.

$\frac{3}{4}$ is an exception to the rule ("Any meter signature whose top number is a multiple of three *excluding three itself* . . ."). There are three beats per measure, and the quarter note receives one beat.

THE CREATIVE PROCESS

Chapter 13 ended with an example (Ex. 13.11) that included a meter signature of $\frac{2}{4}$ and some of the notated rhythms we have worked with in this chapter. If we look at this example again, you should be able to extract the rhythms from the example, using rhythmic syllables to perform the patterns.

When using rhythmic patterns to create music, we must keep the basic ideas of composition in mind. The rhythms used should reinforce the development and resolution of tension in a piece. A sense of rhythmic cadence should be created by using shorter note values ("quicker" notes) to move toward longer note values at resting points. Use rhythm to drive to the cadence points of a composition. Repetition is not limited to melodic patterns only—remember the compositional practice of using rhythmic motives to pull ideas together. This example demonstrates some of these ideas, with repeated rhythms used to tie material together and quicker rhythms moving toward cadence points that use longer note values.

READING ASSIGNMENT

Use rhythm syllables to perform each of the following examples:

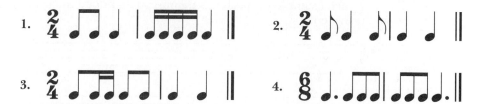

5. (rhythm notation in 6/8)   6. (rhythm notation in 6/8)

WRITTEN ASSIGNMENT

A.

1. On the staff provided, practice notating whole notes. Remember to stay within the space or on the line of the pitch being notated; do not allow the body of the note to extend into another pitch area on the staff.

2. Practice notating half notes and quarter notes.

3. Now practice notating eighth and sixteenth notes. Be sure to include notes that have flags as well as notes that are beamed together. Again, do not be concerned with notating changing pitches; notate the rhythms on one pitch of the staff.

B. Notate each of the rhythm echo patterns for Chapter 1, found on the text tape. Use appropriate quarter notes, dotted quarter notes, and eighth notes in $\frac{2}{4}$ to notate each example properly. Using one pitch, notate the examples on the staff provided.

1.

2.

3.

4.

5.

CREATIVE ASSIGNMENT

Create and notate a rhythm composition in $\frac{2}{4}$. Your composition should utilize the rhythmic patterns we have studied so far and show a clear formal structure. Create a rhythmic period of sixteen measures, moving toward a cadence point in the eighth measure and to a final cadence in the sixteenth measure. You may use one or two quarter notes for the first cadence, but you must use a half note for the final measure. Include in your composition (and indicate in its notation) changes in intensity that are an integral part of the piece. You may wish to refer to previous individual and group creative assignments to guide you in your choice of method and materials.

Do not save this creative assignment on tape but be prepared to perform your composition in class, using your notation as a guide. You may perform the piece using hand claps (and other body sounds if desired), found objects, or a homemade percussion instrument.

JOURNAL ENTRY SUGGESTIONS

As you listen to music during the course of a week, keep a record of meters you hear. How often are duple meters used? How often are triple meters used?

Do you find that most of the music you enjoy listening to has a quick tempo or a slow one? Are there specific rhythmic patterns you find yourself responding to more strongly?

Other Meters

SIMPLE QUADRUPLE METER

Though we have been working exclusively with $\frac{2}{4}$ and $\frac{6}{8}$, rhythmic notation is not limited to these two meters. Similar to the meter of $\frac{2}{4}$ is $\frac{4}{4}$, which also uses a quarter note as its unit of measure. The bottom number of the meter signature tells us this, with its 4 indicating a quarter note. Quarter notes and eighth notes are treated in $\frac{4}{4}$ just as they are in $\frac{2}{4}$. A quarter note is a *du*, and eighths are still paired as *du de:*

Ex. 15.1

The same rhythmic patterns found in a $\frac{2}{4}$ meter are used in $\frac{4}{4}$, but in groupings of four rather than two. Where $\frac{2}{4}$ examples demonstrated simple duple meter, $\frac{4}{4}$ is a *simple quadruple meter*. There is still a feeling of two, but there is a difference in the stress that each note receives. In a simple duple meter like $\frac{2}{4}$ there are only two beats in each measure. The first beat receives the greatest stress, and is the strong beat; the second beat, the weak beat, has less weight. In $\frac{4}{4}$, the first beat again receives the greatest stress and the second beat is weak. Because there are a total of four beats in each measure, however, the third beat has some weight of its own—not as much as the first beat, but more than the weak second and fourth beats. Although both $\frac{2}{4}$ and $\frac{4}{4}$ use the same types of rhythmic patterns, the stress of beats is different and the grouping of rhythms is subtly altered. The following examples compare the treatment of the exact same rhythm, using the two different meters:

Ex. 15.2

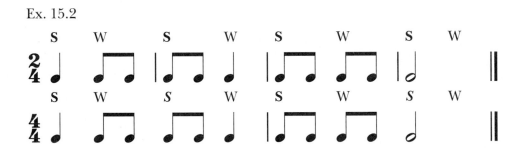

The $\frac{4}{4}$ meter, with four beats to the measure, allows us to notate a whole note. This longer note value can provide a more conclusive final cadence than one in the $\frac{2}{4}$ meter.

Ex. 15.3

With a meter of four we can also combine three quarter notes together into one note, something we could not do in $\frac{2}{4}$. Because this involves grouping in threes, we need to use a dot to show this "odd" number of notes in combination:

Ex. 15.4

$\frac{4}{4}$ 𝅗𝅥. 𝅘𝅥 | 𝅗𝅥 𝅗𝅥 | 𝅗𝅥. 𝅘𝅥 | 𝅝 ‖

CUT TIME

$\frac{2}{4}$ is not the only simple duple meter. Like $\frac{2}{4}$, the meter of $\frac{2}{2}$ has two beats in each measure (the top number of this meter informs us of that). With this new meter, though, the *half note* receives one beat and is the unit of measure. Because the rhythmic value of notes in $\frac{2}{2}$ is half of what they would be in $\frac{2}{4}$, this meter is often referred to as *cut time*.

Ex. 15.5

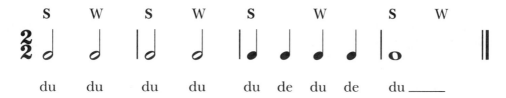

du   du   du   du   du   de   du   de   du _____

With this meter, half notes are *du*'s, and quarter note combinations are performed as *du de*'s. This meter also allows the use of whole notes, either singly or tied together. A *tie* joins two notes together; the total number of beats the note is held is equal to the combined beats of the tied notes.

Example 15.3 would be notated in $\frac{2}{2}$ as follows:

Ex. 15.6

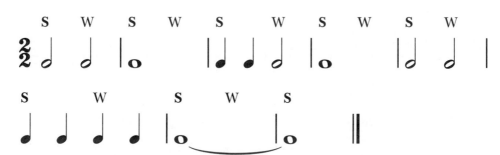

Of course, the above version would differ somewhat from the original example. Rhythmic patterns in $\frac{2}{2}$ are stressed differently from the same patterns in $\frac{4}{4}$. A more direct transference of rhythms happens between $\frac{2}{4}$ and $\frac{2}{2}$, as in both cases the number of beats in each measure remains the same, and the notes of the rhythmic patterns receive the same stresses.

$\frac{2}{2}$ is useful for notating quick and busy rhythms. Many musicians find that more complex rhythms are easier to read in $\frac{2}{2}$. The following example demonstrates this, with a rhythm notated first in $\frac{2}{4}$ and then in $\frac{2}{2}$:

Ex. 15.7

Each of these is in a duple meter, with two beats per measure. The rhythms are the same but are notated differently. In the $\frac{2}{4}$ version, the quarter note is the unit of measure. The $\frac{2}{2}$ rendition of the same rhythm uses the half note as the unit of measure. Though both versions sound the same, the $\frac{2}{2}$ notation avoids sixteenth-note patterns that can be confusing to the eye. $\frac{2}{2}$ was used in the Written Assignment of Chapter 13 to notate "Joy to the World," though the more common notation uses a $\frac{2}{4}$ meter signature.

Ex. 15.8

$\frac{4}{4}$ and $\frac{2}{2}$ are often indicated with the use of the symbols **C** and **¢**, respectively.

Ex. 15.9

Ex. 15.10

The 𝄴 symbol is often referred to as *common time*. Like the *cut time* label for 𝄵, this is a misnomer. Both symbols are actually descended from the early Western church notation of the rhythmic modes. The perfection of the circle (○) was used to indicate a rhythmic mode of three beats, each of which was subdivided into three equal parts. Some contemporary musicians who interpret this early music believe that the "perfect" meter indicated by this symbol was considered better suited to church music, where the mystic number three was held in high esteem. 𝄴, with part of the circle opened, indicated a less perfect meter of four beats subdivided into twos. 𝄵, even further from the perfection of the circle, was used for music with only two beats in a measure, each of which was subdivided into two equal parts.

According to the early Western church, then, the more perfect rhythm modes had three beats in a measure, or had beats that subdivided into groupings of three. The present-day meter of $\frac{6}{8}$, which we've used already, has *two* beats per measure, but each beat subdivides into *three*. Though a simple meter (subdividing each beat into *twos*), $\frac{3}{4}$ has *three* beats in each measure.

SIMPLE TRIPLE METER

We have already seen some examples of music with a meter of three. One of the Written Assignments in Chapter 13 provided us with an example of a $\frac{3}{4}$ melody:

Ex. 15.11

As discussed in Chapter 14 $\frac{3}{4}$ is not a compound meter, but a simple one ("Any meter signature whose top number is a multiple of three (*excluding three itself*) is a compound meter.") The first of three beats in each measure is stressed, and the other two are felt as being progressively weaker. When the music is very fast, however, $\frac{3}{4}$ can be felt in *one* beat subdivided into *three*. The scherzo of Beethoven's Symphony No. 9, with its *presto* tempo, has this feeling:

Ex. 15.12

The rhythm of this example stresses the first beat of each group of three, providing a quick triple feel. We learned when we compared $\frac{4}{4}$ to $\frac{2}{2}$ that the difference between the two meters is found in the stressed beats. The same is true when comparing a *presto* $\frac{3}{4}$ to a piece in $\frac{6}{8}$. Music in $\frac{6}{8}$ has a strong first beat and a weaker second beat. The feeling of this compound meter is

Ex. 15.13

while the same pattern in $\frac{3}{4}$ has a slightly different effect:

Ex. 15.14

As the Beethoven scherzo demonstrates, the use of a quick $\frac{3}{4}$ can provide a strong sense of rhythmic drive. This treatment of the meter, which has occurred throughout the history of Western music, is explored further in Chapter 16, as we learn about the connection between rhythm and melody.

WRITTEN ASSIGNMENT

A. For each pattern, provide rhythmic syllables, then use those syllables to practice performing the example.

1.

B. In the space below each example, renotate the example in $\frac{2}{2}$, providing bar-lines in appropriate places and a double bar at the end.

C. Listen once again to the echo patterns for Chapter 2. Notate the rhythms of Examples 1 through 5, using a $\frac{2}{4}$ meter. Then renotate each of these examples in $\frac{2}{2}$.

JOURNAL ENTRY SUGGESTIONS

What might the development of Western art music have been like if the church believed that five, not three, was the most spiritual number? How would this have influenced the direction of meter development in music?

The Greeks held that different sets of pitches affect listeners in different ways. Could the same be true of different rhythmic patterns? Try to develop some rhythmic modes of your own that seem to have different emotional or spiritual characteristics.

_____

_____

_____

_____

C H A P T E R 16

♪♪♪♪♪♪

Combining Rhythmic and Melodic Elements

So far, we have been studying rhythm and melody separately. There are some benefits to this type of approach, but we also need to understand the connection between these two elements of music.

Earlier forms of music often demonstrated a connection between melody and rhythm in one of two ways: through lyrics or through dance. The poetry of words influenced the rhythms chosen, or the rhythmic necessities of secular dances guided instrumentalists toward specific rhythmic patterns. The rhythmic modes referred to in earlier chapters were a result of these connections.

RHYTHMIC MODES

A historical survey of music shows that short rhythmic patterns were used for entire compositions. The traditional Hebridean song "Taladh Chriosta" ("The Christ Child's Lullaby") uses one rhythm, ♩ ♩, throughout the entire piece.

Ex. 16.1

A rhythmic pattern that begins in a similar fashion,

Ex. 16.2

is seen throughout the fifteenth-century English piece "Agincourt Carol."

Ex. 16.3

The same rhythm is found in the older French chanson "L'Homme Armé."

Ex. 16.4

The rhythmic pattern of "L'Homme Armé" and "Agincourt Carol" is found in music of later years. A 1601 song by Robert Jones, "Now What Is Love," begins with a similar rhythm and also has very close melodic ties to "L'Homme Armé":

Ex. 16.5

Gustav Holst, a twentieth-century English composer, uses this same rhythm in the main theme of his *First Suite in E♭ for Military Band*. This example shows the connection between contemporary music and the older rhythmic modes:

Ex. 16.6

CONTEMPORARY USE OF RHYTHM

Music of later centuries does not always limit itself to the older rhythmic modes. Even so, we often see vestiges of this idea at work in more modern music. Rhythms are combined with melodic motion to provide the basic vocabulary of music. "America" uses one two-measure rhythm for the majority of its melody, with exceptions occurring at cadence points.

Ex. 16.7

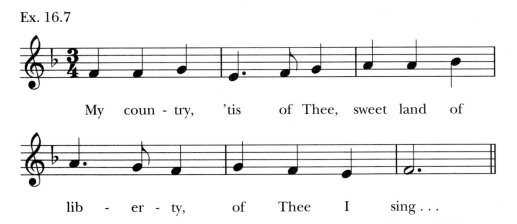

My   coun - try,   'tis   of Thee,   sweet   land   of

lib - er - ty,   of   Thee   I   sing . . .

The words and music of this piece work well with the repeated rhythmic pattern used throughout. The rhythms provide unity in their repetition, while slight changes at cadence points give the melody variety. Though it is true that we may have become accustomed to this particular marriage of melody, lyrics, and rhythms, more than lack of familiarity might make some other rhythmic schemes more difficult to accept. If we change the meter and the basic rhythm pattern, things do not seem to work as well:

Ex. 16.8

My coun-try, 'tis   of Thee, sweet land of lib - er - ty,   of

Thee I sing.   Land where my   fa - thers died, land . . .

Some of these rhythms are suitable, but for the most part the stately flow of the original $\frac{3}{4}$ version is missed. Given the text of the piece, some rhythmic patterns will work, while others will not.

We do not need to have lyrics to make decisions about rhythms. As we saw in the previous chapter, the basic rhythms of the Beethoven scherzo, with no text involved, give the section its drive and melodic momentum. In another movement of the Symphony No. 9 we see simple rhythms used along with conjunct melodic motion to create a folklike melody. The "Ode to Joy" (first seen in examples 13.5 and 13.6) is heard within the last movement of the symphony in a variety of settings, from a simple homophonic presentation to a more complex polyphonic treatment. A chorus and vocal soloists eventually provide lyrics for this melody, but no lyrics are needed for us to appreciate the melding of music's elements in the hands of this great composer.

Ex. 16.9

The simple $\frac{4}{4}$ meter seems natural, as the melody affirms the four-beat patterns with its ascending and descending four-note ideas. The first measure provides the conjunct ascending line, answered by the second measure's descending statement. The third measure helps give unity to the piece, with a sequential version of the first measure. The fourth measure prepares for the cadence with a change in rhythm and a longer note value for the cadence point. This is the first section of a melody that uses rhythm and melodic contour to provide variety as well as necessary repetition.

Simple rhythms are seen in the melody of "Frère Jacques" as well. Exact repetition is used to pair measures together, and rhythmic repetition, with a change in interval, is employed to connect the ending of the piece to measures 3 and 4. $\frac{2}{2}$ is the meter of choice, given the decisions made concerning rhythmic ideas—groupings of two beats dictate this meter signature.

Ex. 16.10

SUMMARY

The use of rhythmic modes is an old concept with new applications. Repeated rhythmic ideas can provide a recurring foundation for a melody and give a sense of balance to a composition. Sometimes a rhythmic motive itself forms the basis for a composition (e.g., Beethoven's scherzo), creating the character and style of the work. Often elements such as lyrics, or extramusical necessities (dance forms or a particular instrument's level of agility) determine the rhythms used in a composition.

Though we have taken a look in this chapter at some basic rhythmic concepts and seen simple examples of those concepts at work, these ideas can serve as resource material for even more complex and demanding compositions. Just as the letters of the alphabet become raw material for written works, simple rhythmic patterns and combinations can be modified, and developed in many different ways. Constant exploration and experimentation with this important element of music can lead us into new and more creative areas of composition.

WRITTEN ASSIGNMENT

A. Choose pitches to use with the rhythmic patterns given and notate them on the staff provided, using treble or bass clef. Practice playing each example at the keyboard or on an instrument of your choice.

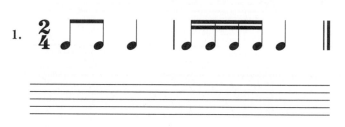

B. Notate each set of pitches, using rhythms of your choice, in the meter given. Perform each example at the keyboard or on an instrument of your choice.

With or without melodic syllables, sing each of the examples found in this chapter. You might also like to play each, using the piano or another instrument.

CREATIVE ASSIGNMENT

Choose one of the following rhythmic modes as a template for an original melodic composition in the key of G. Create a melody of sixteen measures, using the given rhythmic pattern exclusively, except for slight modifications at cadence points. Using traditional notation, notate your result.

JOURNAL ENTRY SUGGESTION

Many amateur and professional musicians find "The Star-Spangled Banner" difficult to sing. Find a printed copy of this piece and determine what the specific problems might be. Use what you know about melody and rhythm to modify the national anthem to create a new and "better" version.

♪♪♪♪♪♪

Sounds of Silence

The creation of original music involves the achievement of a careful balance between opposites like repetition and variety. This balance is important to the development of a logical, coherent musical statement. A primary relationship of opposites in music can be found in the balance between two important ingredients: sound and silence.

THE USE OF SILENCE IN MUSIC

We have discussed the musical characteristics of melody and rhythm and have explored the basic elements of sound production, creation, and re-creation. What has been missing so far is a discussion of the musical element of silence.

It may seem odd to consider silence as a necessary ingredient of good music, but examples from all musical styles and cultures support such an idea. Jazz musicians strive for the proper balance of activity and rest. The phrase "Play the rests" stresses the importance of thinking of rests (beats of silence) as important elements of a good improvised melody. As composers, jazz improvisers recognize the value of silence. Other contemporary composers are aware of the value of silence. John Cage is an example of one composer who has shown great interest in silence as a compositional tool.

In Chapter 8 a notation example that was given demonstrated John Cage's approach to the composition process. The piano part of his Concert for Piano and Orchestra provides only a sketch of the composer's intent. This example shows the composer's tendency to allow the performer greater freedom of interpretation, calling on the pianist to contribute to the creation of the composition. Cage supplies the bare bones of a piece, letting the performer contribute the flesh. As a composer, he values the participation of the performer in the creation of a piece of music.

In addition to allowing the performer to be involved in the creative process, Cage often permits the audience to participate as well. Cage believes that music is not limited to the strict traditions of music reproduction but is an ongoing and ever-changing art form that must allow for "environmental" contributions. The coughing of audience members, the rustling of programs, the intrusion of heater blowers—all are part of the process, and of the music itself. This concept is perhaps most evident in Cage's piece 4'33", a work for piano in three movements. For the duration of the composition (four minutes and thirty-three seconds, or thereabouts) the pianist sits before the keyboard of a piano. He or she remains motionless except to lower and raise the lid of the piano keyboard, signaling the end of one movement and the beginning of the next. At the end of the piece, the pianist stands, takes a bow, and leaves.

With 4'33", Cage has taken the use of silence in music to the highest degree, with a piece composed of nothing but silence. With this composition the composer demonstrates that the sounds of the environment can and should be considered music. It would be impossible for a performance of this piece to be presented with no sound at all occurring—the audience becomes the composer's instrument, its members participants in the process of music making.

RESTS IN MUSIC

Cage's treatment of silence is extreme. Most composers and performers assume that silence is possible, though they may recognize the relative nature of such a state. Musicians realize that silence helps make sense of sound.

Earlier chapters included notated melodies that provide us with examples of silence in music, though we may not have realized this at the time. While most melodies began on the first beat of the first measure, some have one or two notes isolated at the beginning of the piece, coming before the first full measure of music. These examples began with an *anacrusis* (or a *pickup*), a note or a few notes that occur before the first full measure. "The Holly and the Ivy," Written Assignment A1 of Chapter 13, used a quarter note pickup:

Ex. 17.1

The anacrusis indicates that the first measure of music is incomplete—there are beats of silence that precede the first note in "The Holly and the Ivy." It is accepted practice to show only the notes of an incomplete first measure, but any of the following measures that have beats of silence must indicate the silence in relation to the rhythm of the measure. We must notate the silence as accurately as we do the pitches. Just as with the notation of pitch, the notation of silence involves a hierarchy of rhythmic values indicating the specific duration of beats of silence. Just as different note values indicate specific duration, *rests* indicate specific lengths of silence.

Ex. 17.2

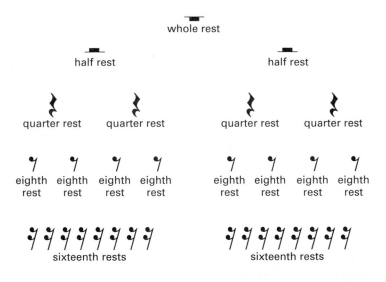

The rests shown, like the note values diagrammed on page 120, start at the whole-note value, and become shorter in duration. The rest at the top of the figure is a *whole rest*. Each whole rest can be broken into two *half rests*. Below the half rests are *quarter rests, eighth rests,* and *sixteenth rests*. In $\frac{4}{4}$, a whole rest "hangs" from the second line from the top of the staff. Half rests, each worth two beats, "sit" on the middle line of the staff. Quarter rests are equal to quarter notes, eighth rests to eighth notes, and sixteenth rests to sixteenth notes. Rests in $\frac{4}{4}$ appear as follows:

Ex. 17.3

The rests indicated in the previous example would be used in music with a simple meter. In a compound meter some rests need to be dotted:

Ex. 17.4

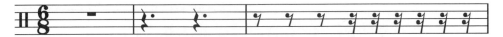

In $\frac{6}{8}$ three eighth rests equal a dotted quarter rest. Two dotted quarter rests can be used in a measure, but it is common practice to use a whole rest instead. Whole rests indicate a full measure of silence no matter what the meter and can be used in $\frac{6}{8}$, $\frac{3}{4}$, and $\frac{2}{2}$ as well as in $\frac{4}{4}$.

Previous examples that began with an anacrusis could indicate the silence before the pickup note or notes through the use of rests:

Ex. 17.5

Ex.17.6

Ex. 17.7

THE CREATIVE PROCESS

In discussing the role of silence in music, we have been dealing with its use in the creative process of music making. Silence can serve to heighten a climax or to create and maintain tension. In presenting a pianist who does not play, John Cage creates tension with silence. He must have known that this tension would lead to audience discomfort and ultimately to audience participation in the creation of 4′33″.

The development of tension and drama is not limited to music that takes such extreme approaches. Rests can bring "space," and help phrases breathe. Cadence points can be created with rests and need not depend exclusively on the use of longer note values. The pauses of rests can help delineate phrases; pickup notes can signal the beginning of a new section or phrase. Silence can enable melodies to be a coherent series of pitches and can bring sense to the presentation of sound in time.

READING ASSIGNMENT

Practice performing each of the following rhythms, using appropriate rhythmic syllables or using an instrument of your choice. The "odd" symbol at the beginning of each example is a neutral clef sometimes used in the notation of music that has rhythms but no pitches.

WRITTEN ASSIGNMENT

A. On the staff provided, practice notating whole rests and half rests. Remember to notate whole rests "hanging" from the second line from the top and half rests "sitting" on the middle line.

B. On the staff provided, practice notating quarter, eighth, and sixteenth rests.

C. Some measures of the following example are incomplete, missing one or more beats. Use half rests and quarter rests to provide the proper number of beats needed in each of these incomplete measures.

D. Use one or more eighth rests to complete the measures that are incomplete in the following example.

CREATIVE ASSIGNMENT

Create an original rhythmic composition for an instrument or ensemble of your choice. Your composition should use a simple meter and be at least sixteen measures in length. Include within your composition examples of each of the rests diagramed on page 144. Use traditional notational practice to notate your composition on staff paper, showing note values on the middle space and notating rests in their proper locations on the staff.

JOURNAL ENTRY SUGGESTIONS

Is it possible to experience complete silence? Is our society comfortable with the idea of silence? Try sitting quietly in as still a space as you can find. What do you hear?

How can silence be used in a piece of music to create tension? To resolve tension?

Comment on any experiences you might have had listening to music that uses the element of silence effectively.

CHAPTER 18

♪♪♪♪♪♪

Further Organization of Melody

We have explored rhythm and melody separately and in tandem. While discovering more about the properties of these two areas of music, we have discussed various ways in which tension is created and resolved, and ways in which melodic material is organized. This chapter deals further with the melodic organization of music, analyzing melodies for specific types of phrases and periods and for ways in which areas of melodies are accented and highlighted.

PARALLEL AND CONTRASTING PERIODS

In Chapter 7 we learned that motives are grouped into phrases, which in turn are combined to form musical periods. Different types of periods are possible, depending on the way in which the phrases are combined.

A simple period is made up of two phrases, an *antecedent phrase,* which "asks a question," and a *consequent phrase,* the "musical answer." The common practice of ending the first phrase on a note other than the tonic gives us the sense of an incomplete statement. The final cadence of the consequent phrase, ending on the tonal center, resolves the musical tension created by the first phrase.

If the consequent phrase of a two-phrase period begins with the same pitches and rhythms as the antecedent phrase, a *parallel period* results. If the consequent phrase uses different material, we have a *contrasting period.*

A parallel period shows an obvious melodic connection between the two phrases, usually in one of the following ways:

1. The consequent phrase is exactly the same as the antecedent phrase, except for a change at the cadence.

Ex. 18.1

2. The consequent phrase begins with the same notes as the antecedent but changes after a short time.

Ex. 18.2

3. The consequent phrase is a sequential or varied repetition of the antecedent phrase (with a change at the cadence).

Ex. 18.3

A contrasting period has a consequent phrase that differs in construction from the antecedent. In a contrasting period, the consequent phrase may use different rhythms and pitches. It may have a contrasting melodic contour—a descending shape that differs from the antecedent's ascending contour, for example. Any type of difference that maintains a connection between the two phrases while showing contrast is possible. The consequent phrase of a period may have the same rhythm as the antecedent phrase, but if the pitches are not the same, the period is considered contrasting, *not* parallel. The consequent phrase of a parallel period must have pitches *and* rhythm in common with the antecedent phrase. An example of a contrasting period follows:

Ex. 18.4

Letters are used to label phrases, with the letter A used for the first phrase. If the second phrase is the same as the first, the same letter is used as a label for the phrase; if the second phrase is a variation of the first, A' is used. The letter B is used for the next phrase, and so on. We saw this system at work in Chapter 7, where we used letters to diagram forms. A simple binary form is labeled A–B, while the label A–B–A is used for ternary structure. It is also common to have an A section, a repeat of the A section, then a change to a B section. The repeat of the A phrase is not heard as a separate section, so an A–A–B structure would still be binary. An A–A–B–A structure would be ternary.

It is sometimes difficult to decide just how long an A section is and where the B section begins. The first phrase of a melody may be four measures long or it may be eight measures. Two phrases may form a period that makes up part I; another two phrases could form part II. This would result in a longer binary form. When making decisions about labeling, we should remember that labels are used to *indicate,* not *determine,* phrases in music. Listen and look for a contrasting section to determine a change in phrase and label it accordingly.

We can now identify periods as contrasting or parallel, and label phrases in a more specific way. This can help us organize our own melodies. As we discovered in earlier chapters, rhythmic values and rests can also play an important role in shaping phrases and cadences. Rests give breathing space, and longer note values help signal the ends of phrases. These elements help outline sections and provide support for the development of a complete musical statement, or period.

ACCENTS

Repetition is important in the process of music listening. For the listener to make sense of music, ideas must be repeated enough for the listener to remember important rhythms, motives, and phrases. Too much repetition, however, can lead to boredom. Composers must use the element of surprise as a contrast to the necessary repetition of ideas. This can give excitement to the piece and provide the music with direction. Unexpected changes and developments also maintain listener interest and keep the audience tuned in to the composition.

There are a number of ways a composer can maintain the listener's interest in a piece. Changing intensity, either suddenly, gradually, or through the terraced addition or deletion of instruments, is one way. Haydn's *Surprise* Symphony has that nickname because of the sudden change in intensity that occurs in the middle of a quiet musical phrase. One note receives an unexpected *accent,* a sudden high level of intensity.

Sometimes accents are built into the piece, and involve elements of music other than intensity. The Beethoven scherzo we heard in Chapter 4 has a steady rhythmic drive, with accented downbeats in each measure of three. In addition to this steady, driving rhythm, Beethoven also provides accented notes within phrases—a few pitches within the melody receive greater emphasis.

Beethoven's "Ode to Joy" theme in his Symphony No. 9 has a much smoother feel compared with the scherzo. We saw a notation of part of this melody in Chapter 16. The complete melody, with its A–A′–B–A′ structure follows:

Ex. 18.5

With this theme, quarter notes are used almost exclusively, and the melody is very conjunct in nature. Repetition is used and there is little to disrupt the flow of rhythmic motion. The one accented area of this melody occurs at the return of the A′. Rather than waiting for the downbeat to begin this final section, Beethoven *anticipates* the first note of the phrase, starting not on the strong first beat but on the weak beat of the measure before. This *accented anticipation,* unexpected as it is, provides the final phrase with a special "lift" that takes the listener by surprise and keeps the theme fresh.

An *accent mark* (>) below the anticipation in the Beethoven example indicates that this note is to be given special emphasis. The accent mark may be interpreted by the performer in a number of ways. The emphasis could be produced through a change in intensity or could be created with a stronger attack. The performer could also interpret the accent with a change of duration, slightly lengthening the accented note.

Because the accent mark gives only a general indication of emphasis, other symbols may be used by the composer to show specific types of changes. An *fp* indication below or above a notehead tells the performer to play the indicated pitch *forte* and immediately drop the dynamic level to *piano.* This dynamic marking was more common in the Classical and Romantic periods of Western music and served as an accent mark that gave a clear indication of intensity change.

Ex. 18.6

A dash above or below a notehead (–) is interpreted by the performer as an *agogic accent.* The note is given emphasis through a slight increase in breath or bow pressure or by a modest lengthening of the pitch. This mark indicates less of an accent than the > symbol.

Ex. 18.7

Other changes in the established routine of a composition can provide variety in the piece. We have heard and seen examples that use changes in timbre to provide interest. We have also seen examples that use changes in texture. Pieces can use modifications of original melodic ideas, elaborating on the rhythms and pitches of the melody. Such *ornamentation* of the original melody provides us with variety while it reinforces the original melodic material. The theme and variations form discussed in Chapter 7 often uses this technique.

Any change in melody, rhythm, form, timbre, texture, or intensity can give a composition spice and help balance repetition and variety. Though the composer may indicate these changes, much is left to the discretion of the performer. Earlier notated music did not include as many indications as modern printed music does. Performance practices were developed by instrumentalists and vocalists to interpret the composer's music as it was meant to be performed. Often, composers were personally involved with the performances of their works and could verbally communicate their wishes to the performers. Standard performance practices developed and were applied to other pieces.

The *messa di voce* is an example of a common performance practice used by vocalists in the early 1600s. The *messa di voce* is an ornamentation produced on a long sustained note. The performer begins the note softly, crescendos, then diminuendos. The indication given in the example below would not necessarily appear in the music of the seventeenth century; the performer would use this technique as a matter of course. We can hear a similar technique used today by classical and pop artists when they start a pitch softly, with no vibrato, and gradually increase the intensity and vibrato.

Ex. 18.8

SUMMARY

In this chapter, we have dealt more specifically with the organization of phrases into periods. We have learned about antecedent and consequent phrases and have seen these phrases used in the construction of parallel and contrasting periods.

We have also seen some of the ways we can add spice and variety to compositions, accenting certain notes or areas in a piece by changing intensity, texture, rhythm, or timbre. In the creation and notation of our own works, we should try to make such changes an integral part of our compositions. The balance of repetition and variety in composition is determined in part by the careful use of elements that add surprise and excitement to a piece, within the context of the work itself.

The performance of notated music requires interpretation, though separating the intentions of the composer from those of the performer can sometimes be difficult. While personal interpretation is necessary for the production of good music, the performer should always strive to discover within the notation of a piece the original desires of the composer. The collaborative effort of composer and performer can help enhance a work and convey the gesture of the music to the listener.

WRITTEN ASSIGNMENT

A. Each example is a period of two phrases. Bracket each phrase, and label each period as *parallel* or *contrasting*.

Type of period:

Type of period:

Type of period:

Type of period:

B. Each example consists of the antecedent phrase of a two-phrase period. Compose a consequent phrase to create a *parallel* period.

antecedent phrase

2.

consequent phrase

antecedent phrase

3.

consequent phrase

C. For each antecedent phrase, provide a consequent phrase that creates a *contrasting* period. For each, use the guidelines provided when creating your answering phrase.

antecedent phrase

1.

consequent phrase—same rhythm, opposite melodic contour

antecedent phrase

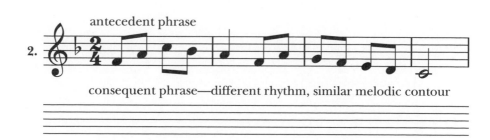

2.

consequent phrase—different rhythm, similar melodic contour

antecedent phrase

3.

consequent phrase—different rhythm, opposite melodic contour

CREATIVE ASSIGNMENT

Create a two-phrase period in the key of G, using a $\frac{4}{4}$ meter. Your period may be parallel or contrasting and should include dynamic marks and at least one accent mark. Remember that all indications in a piece should be an integral part of the work, not just extraneous markings.

You may use one or more rhythm patterns, similar to those used for the Creative Assignment in Chapter 16, or work freely with rhythms of your own choosing.

Notate your composition. Label phrases and indicate the type of period (parallel or contrasting) you have created.

JOURNAL ENTRY SUGGESTIONS

This chapter draws a parallel between speech and music in its description of music's organization of melody. How far can this analogy be taken? How does the organization of music differ from the organization of the written or spoken word? What are the strongest similarities?

In the music you listen to, do lyrics play an important role in determining the structure of melody? If so, in what ways?

PART THREE

♪♪♪♪♪♪

Combining Pitches to Create Chords

In learning about the creation and re-creation of music, we have concentrated on melody and rhythm and their component parts. Chapter 19 explores a new aspect of music: harmony.

Rhythm is the area of music that is concerned with the organization of pulse; melody comprises a coherent series of pitches. Both of these elements of music deal with the *horizontal* aspect of music. Texture begins to involve the vertical aspect of music, but it still deals for the most part with the horizontal movement of pitches. *Harmony* is the element of music that deals with music's *vertical* arrangement of pitches.

Three or more pitches played simultaneously form a *chord*. Chords can be used to accompany a melody, creating harmony. Harmony has been an important aspect of Western music for some time and is certainly prominent in today's popular music. Sometimes harmony serves as motivic material for a composition. The style of music known as "the blues" is based on a standardized progression of chords used as a basic foundation for melodies and improvisation. Chapter 4 showed how rhythm could form the basis of a composition, with rhythmic motives as the vocabulary of a work. The blues and other styles use harmony in much the same way.

BASIC TRIADS

Composed of three notes, the *triad* is the most basic chord. A chord is spelled by using notes in intervals of thirds. The pattern *do mi sol* is one of these.

Ex 19.1

We hear the outline of a chord when these notes are sung or played in series. This melodic presentation of a chord is called an *arpeggio*. If these three pitches are played or sung at the same time, the harmonic presentation of a basic triad results.

Ex. 19.2

Examples 19.1 and 19.2 create a chord by starting with the first note of a major scale. The other notes of the triad are the third and fifth notes of the scale. Whenever we move from the first note of a major scale to the third note of a major scale, the resulting interval is a *major 3rd*. The interval from the first note of a major scale to the fifth note of that scale is a *perfect 5th*. A triad that uses the first, third, and fifth notes of a major scale is a *major triad,* a basic three-note chord with a major quality to the sound.

If we use the first, third, and fifth notes of any major scale, we will have a major triad. Major triads in the keys of G, D, and F are shown here:

Ex. 19.3

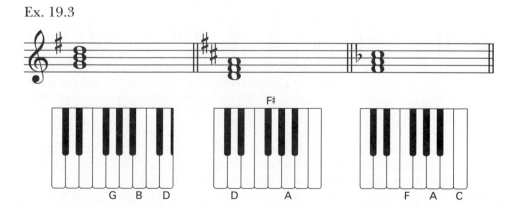

Major triads start with a *root,* or bottom note. From this root we add a major third; a perfect 5th up from the root gives us the last note of our major triad. We can "stack" notes in the same manner, beginning with any note of a major scale, to form other triads. If we have the interval of a major 3rd and a perfect 5th up from the root, we have a major triad. An interval other than a major third or a perfect 5th gives us a triad with a different quality of sound. We will learn more about different types of triads in Chapter 20. For now, we will build triads from each of the notes in a C major scale.

Ex. 19.4

Much folk music, and some pop and art music, uses the chords of one major scale exclusively, with no use of accidentals to shift from the basic tonal center. Music that uses harmony in one key is called *diatonic.* "Lean on Me" is an example of a song that moves from one chord to the next adjacent chord in a major scale. The basic triads are used, with an octave doubling of the root.

Ex. 19.5

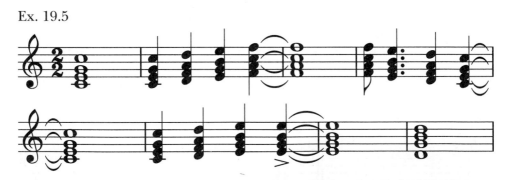

"Lean On Me" (Bill Withers). © 1972 Interior Music.
International copyright secured. All rights reserved.
Used by permission.

Not all music uses chords in this fashion, moving from one triad to the next available chord. More often, specific chords in a key are chosen to be used in a *chord progression.* This concept is discussed in the next chapter.

WRITTEN ASSIGNMENT

A. Practice spelling chords using the given note as the root of a *major* triad. Use whichever of the following two methods is more suited to you:

1. Treat the root as the first note of a major scale. Add the third and fifth notes of the scale to create a major triad.
2. Add the interval of a major 3rd up from the root and then a perfect 5th up from the root, which will result in a major triad.

Below each chord, indicate the position of each note of the chord on the keyboard diagram provided.

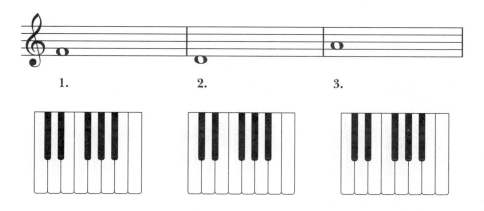

1.   2.   3.

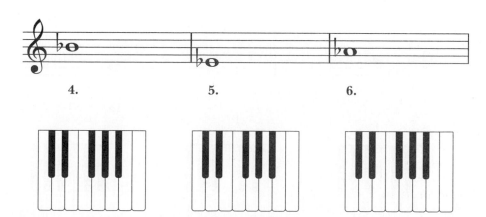

4.   5.   6.

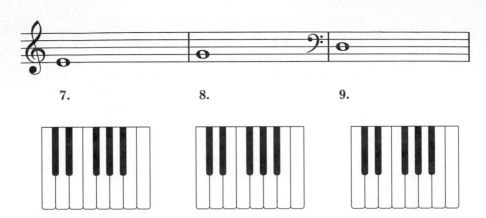

7.   8.   9.

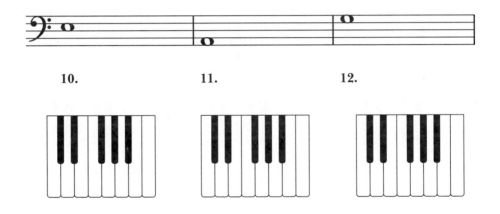

10.   11.   12.

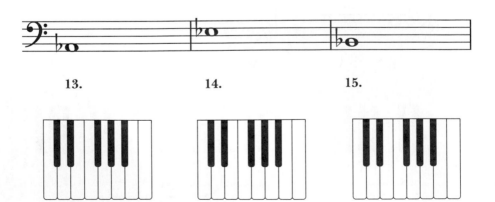

13.   14.   15.

B. On the staff provided, spell basic triads up from each note of the major scale indicated. Be sure to use the necessary sharps or flats required in each key. The first is done for you.

1. Key of D

2. Key of G

3. Key of Bb

4. Key of Ab

5. Key of E

C. Each example has a key signature that indicates a major key. Stack chords up from each note of the major scale indicated by the key signature, starting with the first note of the major scale, and ending with the last. The first is done for you.

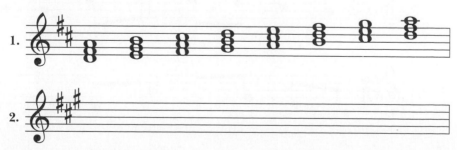

1.

2.

PERFORMANCE ASSIGNMENT

Practice singing each of the patterns below. Many will be familiar to you from the echo pattern examples. Use syllables or a neutral syllable to sing each example; take note of the key signature of each example to establish its tonal center.

CREATIVE ASSIGNMENT

Experiment with the creation of chords that do not stack in thirds. Use a keyboard, a guitar, or another chord instrument to create these "nontraditional" chords. If you play an instrument that produces only one pitch at a time, try singing or humming while you play. What kinds of sonorities can this produce on an instrument that does not traditionally play chords?

Create an original chord collage using the sounds you discover. If you have difficulty producing multiple sonorities on a nonchord instrument, do a multiple-track taping, overdubbing single parts to create a collage.

JOURNAL ENTRY SUGGESTIONS

How much of the music you listen to uses chords? How often does music avoid the use of harmony?

Do you think an instrument that cannot produce chords is more limited than one that can? Does any instrument have the capacity to produce strong melodies *and* chords?

CHAPTER 20

♪♪♪♪♪♪

Harmonic Progression

Harmony involves the use of chords in music. In Chapter 19 we worked with triads in major keys. We also experimented with moving from one note of the major scale to the next, harmonizing each by building up a triad from that note of the scale. Music does not always use chords in this fashion, however. Just as rhythm and melody work in logical, standardized ways, harmony also moves in a logical fashion. This movement seldom takes us through each of the chords of a scale in succession and usually involves only a few of the chords in a major key. The logical movement from one chord to another creates a *harmonic progression*. This chapter explores the concept of harmonic progression.

LABELING CHORDS IN A MAJOR KEY

Musicians commonly refer to chords by using roman numerals. The chord built on the first note of the major scale is called a I chord, while the chord derived from the second note of the scale is called the II chord. This pattern is continued for the entire major scale, so that each chord is named with a specific roman numeral. In the key of C chords are labeled as follows:

Ex. 20.1

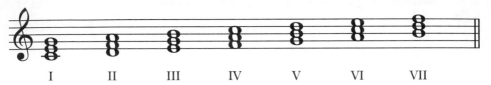

I   II   III   IV   V   VI   VII

The same roman numerals are used in other major keys, with or without key signatures.

Ex. 20.2

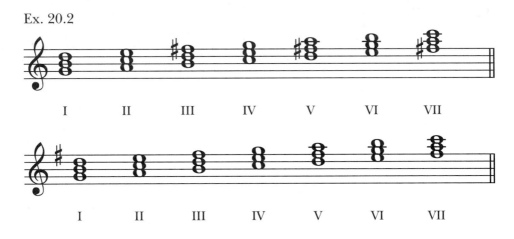

I   II   III   IV   V   VI   VII

I   II   III   IV   V   VI   VII

As mentioned in Chapter 19, some of the chords built from notes in a major scale are major chords; others are not. In any major key, the chords that are major in quality are the I chord, the IV chord, and the V chord.

Ex. 20.3

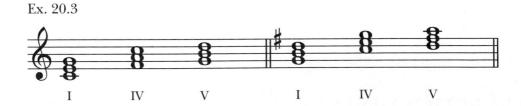

I   IV   V   I   IV   V

HARMONIC PROGRESSIONS

Harmonic progressions in major keys use I, IV, and V chords to a great extent because the major quality of these chords supports the tonality of music in major keys. A simple harmonic progression in a major key is I–IV–V–I. The tonal center of the major key is established and reaffirmed not just with the tonic chord but through the process of the complete chord progression. The tonic is established with the I chord; tension is created by moving to the *subdominant* IV chord, which in turn prepares the *dominant* V chord. The V chord, containing the seventh scale degree of *ti*, pulls home to the I chord. The return to the tonic chord completes the harmonic progression and resolves the tension.

Ex. 20.4

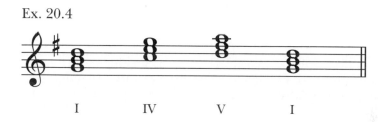

     I   IV   V   I

    This progression uses *root position* chords. The chords are presented as they were first created, from the root up. This root-position progression, however, undermines the tendency of *ti* to move to *do*. The V chord has *ti* located too far from *do* and does not provide us with the half-step motion that should be outlined. The use of chords in a harmonic progression is not just a vertical arrangement; the notes in chords must be treated in a melodic fashion as well. This involves the rearrangement of notes in the chords, so that melodic tendencies like *ti* to *do* are reinforced. The I–IV–V progression of Example 20.4 could be rewritten as:

Ex. 20.5

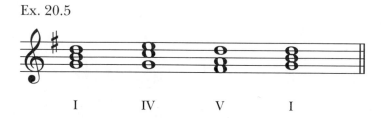

     I   IV   V   I

    The notes of the IV and V chords in Example 20.5 are the same as those in Example 20.4 but are rearranged to enhance the melodic tendencies of the I–IV–V–I progression. When we move from the I chord to the IV chord, we keep the tonic as the lowest note of the IV chord. The rest of the IV chord pitches are then notated above this tonic note, an octave higher than they appeared when the chord was in root position. When we move to the V chord, we move as smoothly as possible, using conjunct motion when we can. We move from *do* **down** to *ti*, setting up the pull back to the tonic. The other notes of the V chord are filled in above *ti*, giving us the arrangement of Example 20.5. Moving from the V chord back to I, we have one note in common—*sol.* The other pitches resolve up, with *ti* moving to *do*, and *re* to *mi*.

Example 20.5 provides one example of a I–IV–V–I progression. Other arrangements that maintain the melodic tendencies of the notes in the chords and that move smoothly from one chord to the next are possible.

HARMONIC CADENCES

Harmonic progressions supply harmony for melodies, establish tonality, and create and resolve tension. Chord progressions contribute to the sense of movement toward a cadence. A halfway point is reached in a harmonic progression ending with the V chord. A resting point on a V chord is a *half cadence*.

Ex. 20.6

A *full cadence* resolves to the I chord.

Ex. 20.7

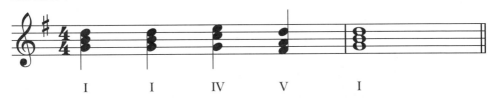

Harmonic progressions can be used in conjunction with melody and rhythm to provide music with cadences. The first phrase of a melody, ending on a note other than the tonic, ends with a chord other than the I chord. The final cadence, with the tonic in the melody, is supported by a I chord. Harmony is closely associated with rhythmic and melodic motion, and chords must be chosen with care. Chord progressions must move not only vertically but horizontally, supporting the melodic motion of a piece of music. The art and craft of harmonizing a melody is discussed in detail in Chapter 21.

PERFORMANCE ASSIGNMENT

Practice singing (arpeggiating) a I–IV–V–I chord progression in the major keys you know. Use singing syllables or a neutral syllable with the melodic pattern given, or use a pattern of your own choosing.

WRITTEN ASSIGNMENT

A. Spell the chords indicated in the given major keys, in root position. Examples 1 and 2 do not have key signatures; be sure to use the sharps or flats needed for each chord. Practice playing each of the chords at a keyboard, with a guitar, or using another chord instrument.

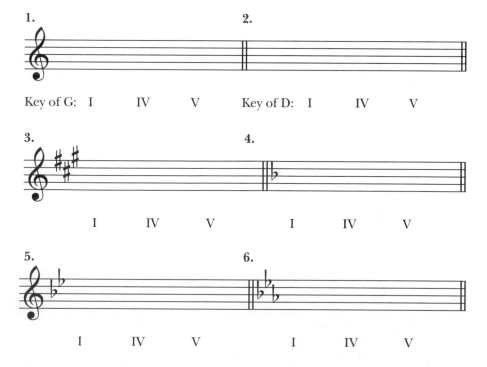

B. Practice writing I–IV–V–I progressions in the given keys. Start with the given tonic chord in root position, then spell a subdominant chord by keeping the tonic in the same position and filling in the rest of the IV chord pitches an octave above their usual location. The dominant chord will have *ti* as its bottom note, with the other notes of the chord above. Refer to the root position IV and V chords of Written Assignment A to check pitches, and to Example 20.5 for the pattern used in this version of the progression. The examples do not have key signatures; be sure to use the sharps or flats needed for each chord. Practice playing these progressions at the keyboard when you have finished. The first is done for you.

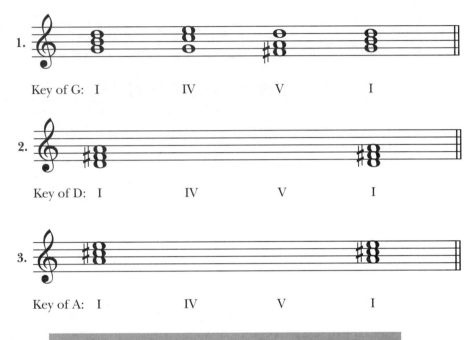

1. Key of G: I   IV   V   I

2. Key of D: I   IV   V   I

3. Key of A: I   IV   V   I

JOURNAL ENTRY SUGGESTION

Performing musicians use a standard pitch to tune. Presently, the pitch used for tuning is an A that vibrates at 440 cps (440 cycles per second). Some time ago, the A used for tuning might have been 380 cps. What might be some reasons for the change in the standard of tuning?

_____

_____

_____

_____

CHAPTER 21

♪♪♪♪♪♪

Harmonizing Melodies

We have practiced spelling some basic triads and have begun to understand how chords work in harmonic progressions. Chord progressions are seldom isolated events, however. Harmony works in conjunction with melody and rhythm, and part of the process of developing progressions is making decisions about which specific chords work with particular melody notes.

CHOOSING CHORDS FOR HARMONY

The reasoning used in Chapter 20 to develop the I–IV–V–I progression can serve as a model in making decisions about the harmonization of melodies. We can analyze a melody for the same patterns and motion that was important in developing a harmonic progression. If the first phrase of a melody ends on a note other than the tonic, some chord other than the I chord will be used for harmony. If we have a full cadence at the end of the second phrase, a tonic chord would be appropriate. Even if we limit ourselves to a few chords like I, IV, and V, we will have many possibilities for chord progressions that support and enhance melodies.

Chapter 19 introduced us to chord structure with the presentation of the familiar *do mi sol* melodic pattern (Example 19.1). This *arpeggio* uses all of the notes of a tonic chord. In Example 19.1 the I chord is outlined in this short melodic pattern; this chord could be used as harmony for the duration of the arpeggio.

Melodies we wish to harmonize can have patterns that outline chords. This can make the process of choosing chords for progressions much easier—we can analyze the melody for implied harmony, looking for arpeggiated chords.

Ex. 21.1

a.

b.

c.

Each of the melodies above outlines a I chord (where bracketed). Where the tonic chord is outlined, a I chord would be used for harmony. Similar instances of outlined chords may indicate the use of a IV chord or a V chord. Harmonic and melodic motion are often joined in this way, with the movement from the tonic to the subdominant or dominant revealed in the melody itself.

Ex. 21.2

Example 21.2 uses implied I, IV, and V chords. Harmonic changes are outlined in the notes of the melody itself, making the process of harmonization much easier. Such obvious indications of harmony are not always the case, however. In choosing chords for a melody, we may need to analyze the melody more carefully to make decisions about which chords will be used.

As seen in the melodies of Examples 21.1 and 21.2, disjunct melodies often outline chords. On the other hand, with their scalewise motion, conjunct melodies do not provide us with obvious chord choices. We must take some further steps to choose the proper chords and their placement in the melody. When analyzing conjunct melodies, we need to determine which notes are most important and how often we need to change chords. If we plan on using the basic I, IV, and V chords, we can look at each note of the melody to see which chord could be used. This can be a first step in deciding which chords will be used for harmonization. Applying this process to a portion of Beethoven's "Ode to Joy," we can list the possible chords for each of the notes in the melody. The root position, I, IV, and V chords are given at the beginning of the example as a reference, and chord possibilities are listed for each melody note.

Ex. 21.3

In most cases, only one chord is possible for harmonization. In just four instances, two chords can be chosen from. We must further decide how often we need to use a different chord—we may not need to change as frequently as every beat. We need some other tactics to help us make this decision.

The tempo of a piece of music can tell us how quickly the harmonic progression should move. A slow piece changes chords more frequently than a quick selection, though neither may need to move to a different chord every time the melody note changes. The Beethoven example moves quickly (about allegro), and we may find that a chord change on every note becomes cumbersome, slowing down the momentum of the melody. The melody is moving quickly enough so that notes that do not fit into a particular chord are heard in passing. In the first measure of the "Ode to Joy," the G is the only note that does not fit into a I chord. We could try to use a I chord for the entire measure, treating the G as a passing tone. A *passing tone* is a nonchord tone (a note not found in the chord) that is approached by a step and moves stepwise in the same direction toward another chord tone. The same could be done with the G and E in the second measure, and the E in measure 3. We would then use a I chord for all of the melody, except for the last two notes, where a half cadence is implied and where the only choice for harmony is a V chord.

Ex. 21.4

I   IV   V   I   V

   This harmonization is one possibility. We could change chords more frequently, choosing to change chords when more than one chord is possible. We need to keep in mind the needs of the harmonic progression, being sure to move from the tonic, creating tension, cadencing (half or full), and eventually resolving back to the tonic. Logic alone can bring us to this point, but we must also use our ears to make the final decision about which chords to use and how often to change chords. Listening carefully as we try different combinations will help us in harmonization. If we combine this listening process with an analysis of cadential needs, a search for outlined chords in the melody, and a listing of possible chord choices, we will be able to make intelligent decisions about harmonizing our melodies.

NOTATING HARMONIZATIONS

Once we have decided which chords will be used in our harmonization and how often chord changes will occur, we can use what we have learned about moving smoothly from one chord to the next to notate our harmonization. We can use a grand staff, notating the melody in the treble staff and the harmony in the bass. This allows us to play the melody with the right hand and the harmony with the left at the keyboard. We could use this procedure to notate Example 21.4:

Ex. 21.5

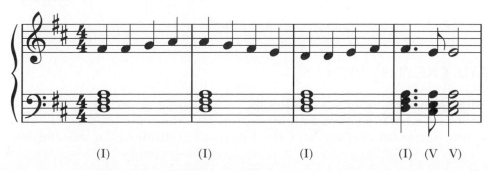

        (I)   (I)   (I)   (I) (V V)

We have notated the harmonic changes, using the simplest rhythm for the left-hand chords. We could change the character of the harmony, and of the piece, by changing the rhythm of the accompanying chords:

Ex. 21.6

By making this slight change in the rhythm of the harmony, without changing the chords used, we have altered the feeling of rhythmic motion. The rhythmic pattern used helps provide some rhythmic repetition to the harmonic progression and gives it a character of its own. Example 21.6 illustrates the strong connection between melody, harmony, and rhythm in a work, a symbiotic relationship that must be respected when dealing with one or another of the elements of musical composition.

We could follow the same procedure with another harmonization of Beethoven's melody, using a different chord progression and a different rhythmic pattern:

Ex. 21.7

THE CREATIVE PROCESS

We have a number of possibilities for harmonizing a melody, even one as basic and uncomplicated as "Ode to Joy." We must use all that we know about harmony, melody, and rhythm to help guide us in making our choices. We must also use our aural abilities to listen discriminately deciding what "sounds right." While making our decision, we may lean toward a simple harmonization, or we may wish to experiment with different chords. As with other aspects of music creation, we must carefully balance the proven with the experimental. Continued work with chord progressions and harmonization of melodies will increase our exposure to different possible combinations and develop our harmonic vocabulary.

WRITTEN ASSIGNMENT

A. Each example contains outlined I chords. Use a bracket to indicate where the chords are arpeggiated in the melody and label them with a roman numeral I. Practice singing each example, using singing syllables or a neutral syllable to perform each.

B. The following examples also have arpeggiated chords. In addition to I chords, some may have IV chords or V chords. Follow the same procedure for these examples as with Written Assignment A, bracketing and labeling chords, then singing the melodies.

Traditional English, "Harry the Tailor"

Traditional English, "The Long and Wishing Eye"
(B section)

Traditional French carol, "Il est né le Divin Enfant"

C. Harmonize each melody, choosing appropriate chords and providing accompaniment in the bass staff. Be sure to play the examples at a keyboard.

1.

2.

CREATIVE ASSIGNMENT

Harmonize a new original melody or one you had previously created in the key of G major. Use I chords, IV chords, and V chords for your harmony. Notate the melody on a treble staff, with the harmonization on the bass staff. Use good-melodic motion between chords, be creative with accompaniment rhythms, and be sure to move toward cadence points.

JOURNAL ENTRY SUGGESTION

If you had to rank melody, harmony, and rhythm, which would you consider the most important in music? Which would be the least important? Why?

CHAPTER 22

♪♪♪♪♪♪

The V^7 Chord

In dealing with harmony, we have been using the basic major triads of the major scale. Chords comprise at least three notes, but they are not limited to just that number of pitches. We can extend the triads we have been using through the addition of other notes. Continuing the "stacking" process past the root, third, and fifth of the chord gives us a 7th. A 7th can be added to any triad; we will be working in this chapter with a common seventh chord, the V^7.

The V chord has a root, and, from that bottom note, the interval of a major 3rd and a perfect 5th. If we add the interval of a *minor* 7th up from this root, we create a V^7 chord. This minor 7th is a half step lower than the major 7th interval.

Ex. 22.1

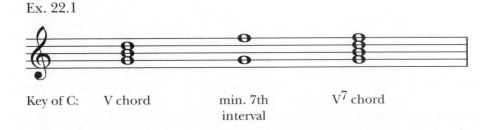

Key of C: V chord   min. 7th V^7 chord
                         interval

THE TRITONE

Contained within the V^7 chord is the interval of a tritone. As we discussed in Chapter 10, this is a dissonant interval. Its use in the V^7 chord creates tension and a sense of instability that are used to advantage in harmonic progressions.

Ex. 22.2

The interval from B to F is that of a tritone. What is significant about this interval is the fact that each pitch is a minor 2nd away from a note in the I chord. The B pulls to the tonic C, and the F pulls down to the third of the tonic chord, E. This creates an even stronger sense of V resolving to I.

Ex. 22.3

V^7 I

We can see this same melodic tendency in other major keys, moving V^7 to I:

Ex. 22.4

V^7 I V^7 I

The melodic tendencies of the tritone within the V^7 chord must be maintained in its use in harmonic progressions. With the I–IV–V–I progression, we saw that movement from one chord to the next is a horizontal process as well as a vertical one. The *ti* of the V chord should resolve to *do* in the I chord. With the V^7 chord, we have the additional restriction created by the tritone. The seventh of the chord, *fa*, must resolve down to *mi* in the I chord.

THE V⁷ CHORD IN HARMONIC PROGRESSIONS

Because of the melodic tendencies of the tritone, the cadence of V^7 to I is even stronger than a full cadence that uses the V triad without the seventh. The tension created by the tritone and the natural tendency of this interval to resolve to the root and third of the tonic chord provide a very conclusive full cadence. The unstable quality of the chord precludes its use in a half cadence—a V triad should be used when ending a phrase on the V chord. V^7 to I can be used for a strong full cadence.

Ex. 22.5

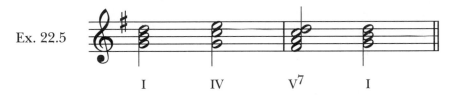

    I   IV   V⁷   I

We can isolate the notes of the chords to show melodic motion within the progression:

Ex. 22.6

    I   IV   V⁷   I   I   IV   V⁷   I   I   IV   V⁷   I

We can see the conjunct motion that is created and reinforced within the basic I–IV–V^7–I progression. Historically, the progression had its origins in the melodic motion of one pitch to the next. This is especially true of the development of the V^7 chord. The seventh of the V^7 chord began as a passing tone, starting on the root of the chord, moving down to the seventh, and continuing down, resolving to the third of the I chord:

Ex. 22.7

    I   V   (V⁷)   I

The seventh of the V⁷ chord can be presented rhythmically with the rest of the pitches in the chord, but the resulting tritone still requires careful preparation. The seventh must still be approached by a step, making the motion to and from the dissonant interval as smooth as possible.

Ex. 22.8

I   IV   V⁷   I

Example 22.8 uses a grand staff. This allows the root of each chord to be presented as the bottom note, while the treble staff pitches move conjunctly. You may notice that a note is missing from the V⁷ chord in this example. To create smooth motion from one chord to the next, the fifth of the V⁷ chord is omitted. The sound of the chord is not drastically affected when this is done, because the "important" notes of the chord are still in place. The root and third of the chord provide the chord with its basic major quality, and the interval of the tritone is present. If you play the progression at the keyboard, first with the fifth or the V⁷ and then without, you will notice very little change in the sound of the progression.

OTHER SEVENTH CHORDS

When we stack a seventh on top of a V chord, we create a seventh chord on the *dominant* chord of a major key. The resulting *dominant seventh chord* has a particular sound because of the interval of the tritone. If we start with any major triad and add the interval of a minor 7th up from the root, we will have the sound of a dominant seventh chord, even if the chord is not a V chord. Altering the top note of the major 7th interval by lowering the top pitch a half step provides us with the interval of a minor 7th. In the example below, the major 7th interval from the given pitch D, the C♯, is altered by lowering the C♯ to a C. Adding this pitch to the major triad gives us a dominant seventh chord.

Ex. 22.9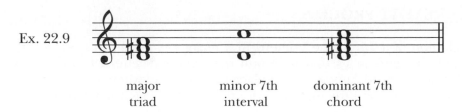

major   minor 7th   dominant 7th
triad   interval   chord

We could create dominant seventh chords from the I chord and the IV chord, in addition to the V chord, if we add a minor 7th up from the root of each chord:

Ex. 22.10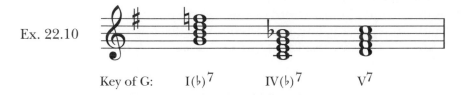

Key of G: I(♭)⁷   IV(♭)⁷   V⁷

We can use the popular practice of referring to chords with a dominant seventh sound with just the "7th" indication. This implies the added interval of a minor 7th, something that happens automatically on the V chord and that requires an accidental on other chords.

The I⁷, IV⁷, and V⁷ chords of Example 22.10 are used in the blues progression mentioned in Chapter 19. This progression uses these dominant seventh chords in a standardized sequential pattern. A complete blues progression in a meter of four takes twelve measures to complete. The basic pattern is as follows (though variations, of course, are possible):

Ex. 22.11

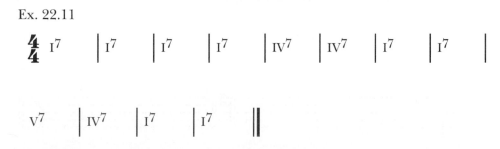

This basic blues progression can be played in any major key. With this progression we find less of a melodic approach to the use of dominant seventh chords. Resolution of the tritone is not an issue, and the sound of one dominant seventh chord followed by another is more important than the melodic tendencies of individual pitches. This harmonic pattern serves as a basic source for improvised melodies and creates a style of music with a very individual character. This progression is used today not only in the blues, but in rock and roll and other styles as well.

THE CREATIVE PROCESS

The addition of a 7th to the V chord in a major key results in a V^7 chord with melodic tendencies that help pull the dominant chord to the tonic chord. The V^7 chord can be used in place of the V triad when a stronger full cadence is desired or if the melody seems to imply this extended chord.

In more modern music, especially popular styles, the dominant seventh chord is used more freely. Dominant sevenths may stand on their own, used for the sound they produce, with less concern given to the melodic tendencies of the individual pitches. The blues progression that uses the dominant seventh sound of the I, IV, and V chords is one application of this idea. Other uses of dominant seventh chords are possible.

The dominant seventh chord is one possible extension of the basic major triad. Other triads and other types of 7ths can provide different types of seventh chords, used in a variety of ways. Chapter 23 explores these other seventh chords.

WRITTEN ASSIGNMENT

A. For each major key, notate a V^7 chord. After providing the complete dominant seventh, outline the tritone interval found between the third and seventh of the chord and show the resolution of this interval to the root and third of the tonic chord. The first is done for you.

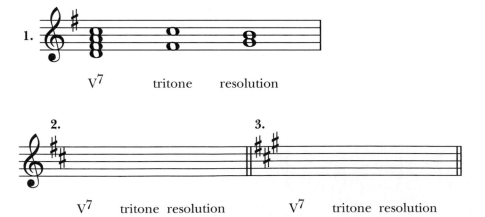

B. Practice spelling dominant seventh chords outside a major key. Use the given pitch as the root of a dominant seventh chord and spell a major chord with the addition of the interval of a minor 7th from the root. The first is done for you.

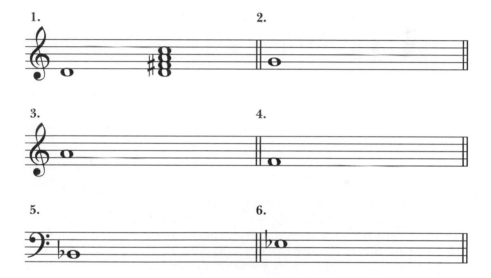

C. For each example, complete the chord progression in the major key indicated by the key signature. The I chords and the bass line are given for each. The first is done for you.

D. Reharmonize a Chapter 21 melody of your choice, using V^7 chords in place of V chords, except where the V chord is the final chord of a half cadence.

E. Harmonize the given melody, using I chords, IV chords, and V chords. Use V^7 chords where possible (*not* at a half cadence). Provide the notated harmony in the bass staff, creating smooth motion between chords. Below the bass staff, give the roman numerals of the chords you have chosen for your harmonization.

CREATIVE ASSIGNMENT

Create an original harmonic progression that serves as a basic compositional motive. Experiment with combinations of basic triads and dominant seventh chords. Be aware of the importance of rhythm to the compositional process. Use rhythm in conjunction with chord repetition to provide your composition with balance and continuity.

JOURNAL ENTRY SUGGESTION

The chord progression known as the blues seems to have developed on its own terms. Do we find the same melodic tendencies and resolutions in the blues that we find in more traditional progressions that use dominant seventh chords? Do the seventh chords in the blues progression resolve in the traditional manner? What gives the blues its unique sound?

How many different styles of music can you identify that seem to use the blues progression or a variation of it?

CHAPTER 23

♪♪♪♪♪♪

Other Extended Chords

We have learned about I chords, IV chords, and V chords in major keys. These chords have formed the basis of our study of harmony so far, but they are not the only ones we can use when harmonizing a melody. Any chord formed in the major scale can be used for harmony, keeping in mind that a harmonic progression is the desired result of using chords. The I–IV–V–I progression sets up the tonic, pulls away, and comes back, giving us the most basic of harmonic progressions. We can use some other chords in major keys to provide us with variations of this harmonic motion.

MINOR CHORDS IN MAJOR KEYS

The I chord, IV chord, and V chord are all major. These are the major chords found in a major key. Chords built on other notes in the scale have a different quality of sound. The ii chord, iii chord, and vi chord are all *minor*. Whereas a major triad has the interval of a major 3rd up from the root and a perfect 5th up from the root, the minor triad uses a *minor 3rd* and a perfect 5th. The use of the minor 3rd gives the chord its minor sound.

The interval of a minor 3rd results when we lower the top note of a major 3rd one half step. The first and third notes of a D major scale create a major 3rd. Lowering the F♯ to an F results in the interval of a minor 3rd.

The *natural sign* is the accidental used to cancel a previous sharp or flat and is used in the example for the notation of D to F:

Ex. 23.1

major 3rd   minor 3rd

If we add to our minor 3rd the interval of a perfect 5th from the root, we will have a minor triad:

Ex. 23.2

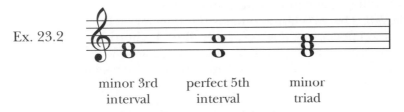

minor 3rd   perfect 5th   minor
interval   interval   triad

This minor chord built up from a D is the ii chord in the key of C. When we use the notes of the C major scale to create chords, stacking up from the D gives us the notes of a D minor triad. You can play this chord at a keyboard and compare it with the sound of the major triad built on the same root.

Other triads in a major key are "naturally" minor in sound. As we move up the C major scale, the iii chord is the next minor triad to be produced. This chord contains the interval of a minor 3rd up from the root and a perfect 5th up from the root. The resulting sound is that of a minor triad.

Ex. 23.3

Key of C:

The vi chord is also minor.

Ex. 23.4

Key of C:

If we were to compare the spelling of this chord with the spelling of the I chord in A major, we would see the difference:

Ex. 23.5

Key of A: I   Key of C: vi

With the ii chord, the iii chord, and the vi chord, lowercase roman numerals are used to indicate that these chords are minor in sound, not major. Lowercase roman numerals are used for the vii° chord as well, but a small circle is also used when this chord is indicated. This circle indicates that the chord is *diminished*. The vii° chord contains the interval of a tritone. Because this interval is also known as a *diminished fifth*, the vii° chord is called a *diminished triad*. When forming a vii° chord, we create a minor 3rd up from the root of the chord, and a tritone, or diminished 5th, up from the root as well:

Ex. 23.6

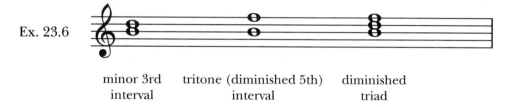

minor 3rd   tritone (diminished 5th)   diminished
interval   interval   triad

We find ii chords, iii chords, vi chords, and vii° chords at work in some harmonic progressions. I–vi–ii–V–I is a common progression that uses two of these triads.

THE I–vi–ii–V–I PROGRESSION

We have already learned that a specific harmonic progression can serve as basic material for a composition. The blues progression discussed in Chapter 22 is an example of this. In jazz, and in rock and pop music of certain styles and eras (especially the 1950s and 1960s), another chord progression serves as the raw material for numerous compositions: I–vi–ii–V–I.

The I–vi–ii–V–I progression, sometimes called the ii–V progression, begins and ends just like the standard I–IV–V–I, with the tonic. Both progressions also use the V chord as the penultimate sonority. The ii–V chord progression uses the vi chord followed by the ii chord in place of the basic progression's IV. The vi chord seems to move naturally to the ii chord, and the ii chord, in turn, sets up the V. The movement of the roots of these chords might have something to do with this.

The strong pull of the V chord to the I chord is due, in part, to the movement from *sol* to *do* of the roots of the chords. In the key of C, the pitch G as a bass note moves readily back to C, or *do*:

Ex. 23.7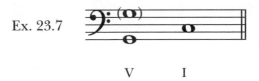

V   I

The ii–V progression has three of these root movements of a 5th (or 4th, if displaced an octave):

Ex. 23.8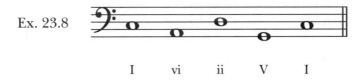

I   vi   ii   V   I

The A bass note of the vi chord is a temporary "sol" to the D bass note of the ii chord. This D, in turn, sets up the G of the ii chord. Finally, we come home to the tonic chord, with a final pull from G to C. The root motion of 4ths and 5ths moving vi–ii–V–I is very strong and is an extension of the V–I cadence idea. The completed harmonic progression, with root position chords and a keyboard-style right-hand arrangement of chord tones, is given here:

Ex. 23.9

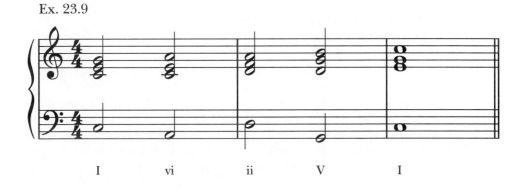

I   vi   ii   V   I

Except for the movement from V to I, as we move from one chord to the next at least one note is held in common, while the other notes move conjunctly. This gives the ii–V progression a "smooth" sound. If we substitute a V^7 chord for the V triad, we will have an even smoother movement from ii to V, with the seventh of the V^7 chord having its beginnings as a chord tone of the ii chord.

Ex. 23.10

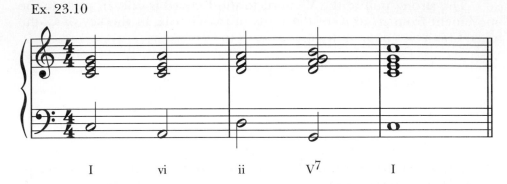

I   vi   ii   V⁷   I

The addition of the seventh to the V chord helps give a final pull to the tonic but also sets the chord apart from all the others. We now have the strong root movement in fifths *throughout* the progression, and the added spice of the seventh of the V⁷ chord helps set the final cadence apart from the rest of the progression.

The ii–V progression has been used as the basis for a number of compositions. If you have tried to play through the progression, you may have found yourself recalling one or more of these melodies. "Heart and Soul" is one of many songs that uses this harmonic progression.

As with the blues, the ii–V serves as a standard progression that composers use as source material for original melodies. We do not need to limit ourselves to just this standardized use of ii chords and vi chords, however. We could try to incorporate these chords into the harmonization of other melodies as well.

USING ii CHORDS AND vi CHORDS IN HARMONIZATIONS

With our introduction to ii chords and vi chords and their uses in harmonic progression, we have increased our harmonic vocabulary. We can now try to apply what we know to the harmonization of existing melodies. If we combine logic with careful listening, we can use these new chords in the same way we have used IV chords and V chords in harmonic progressions. We will apply this to the familiar "Ode to Joy" melody of Beethoven. Given here are the chords we will be using, in the key of D:

Ex. 23.11

I   ii   IV   V   vi

In preparing to reharmonize the melody, let's first list all possible chords for each of the melody notes in the first phrase, keeping our new ii and vi chords in mind as possibilities:

Ex. 23.12

As we make choices about which chords to use for harmonizing, we must think about root and chord movement and follow the natural tendencies of the melody. Some possibilities will be more feasible than others. We probably would not want to begin the piece with a vi chord, for example. It would be better to establish the tonality of the composition with the tonic I chord. The harmony for the half note E has two possibilities—a V chord or a ii chord. Because this is a cadence point, the ii chord would not be a logical choice.

Other combinations will not lend themselves to a harmonic progression and may be eliminated as possibilities. Moving from ii to vi in the beginning of the second measure is an option but not one that moves the harmony in a forward direction. We could, however, create a I–vi–ii–V pattern in the first measure or the second measure. We could also take advantage of this possibility for the cadence in the fourth measure. With our increased harmonic vocabulary, then, we have some other options besides just I, IV, or V chords.

We must keep in mind at least two other ideas as we reharmonize Beethoven's melody. The style of the melody is one of these. The "Ode to Joy" theme is folklike; a complex-sounding harmony would not be in keeping with the character of the piece. We must be careful with our use of the "fancier-sounding" vi and ii chords in our progression.

We should also remember that a balance of repetition and variety is necessary. If we use too many vi chords and ii chords in our progression, they will lose some of their impact. Just as Beethoven saved the accent for one particular spot in his melody, we must try to use the more exotic-sounding ii and vi chords with care. With greater freedom of choice comes greater difficulty of composition. Experiment with some possible combinations of chords to see which seem to sound best.

OTHER EXTENSIONS OF HARMONY

In the previous chapter, we extended the V chord with the use of an additional note, the 7th. The use of a 7th to extend a chord is not limited to the V chord. Other chords can be extended in a similar fashion.

If we were to add a note to the pitches in a ii chord, we would have a 7th chord, but one with a different sound from the V^7. In both cases, the added interval up from the root is a minor 7th, but the ii chord's basic *minor* triad works with this added interval to create the sound of a *minor seventh chord*. The intervals up from the root are a minor 3rd, a perfect 5th, and a minor 7th:

Ex. 23.13
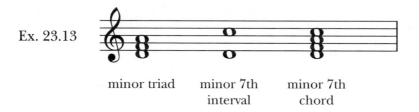

minor triad   minor 7th   minor 7th
            interval   chord

Anytime a minor 7th is added to a minor triad, a minor seventh chord is the result. If we add a *major 7th* to a *major* triad, we have a *major seventh chord*. In the key of C, the I chord and the IV chord can be extended to become major seventh chords:

Ex. 23.14
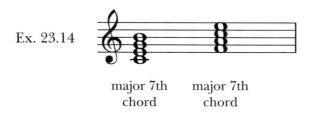

major 7th   major 7th
   chord   chord

We can use "jazz/pop" chord symbols to show these extended chords. Remember that a "7" indicates a *dominant* 7th chord; we need to be more specific if we are to indicate a major or minor seventh chord. In the key of C, extended chords will be shown as given in Example 23.15:

Ex. 23.15

Cmaj7   Dm7   Em7   Fmaj7   G7   Am7   Bm7♭5

Major triads with major 7th intervals added are labeled *maj7*. Minor seventh chords use the abbreviation *m7*. The dominant seventh sound of the V^7 chord is indicated in the key of C as G7. Notice that the jazz/pop indication for a diminished chord with an added 7th is "minor 7th, flat 5th." The chord is labeled a minor seventh chord with the change of a flatted fifth.

THE CREATIVE PROCESS

Major seventh and minor seventh chords give a different flavor to harmonies. Many jazz performers use these extended chords, and use even further extensions of elevenths and thirteenths to create a richer-sounding harmony. Though you will seldom hear these chords used to harmonize simpler folk melodies (or folk-style melodies like Beethoven's "Ode to Joy"), they are sometimes used to give a different flavor to the sound of the melody. The final recorded example on the text tape, "The Water Is Wide," is a folk melody that has been harmonized with standard chords for the first verse. Another verse is given, this time with extended chords used for the harmonization. Included in this reharmonization is a Cmaj9 chord, which uses the major 7th and the major 9th extensions of the C major tonic chord. Other "jazz" chords that provide extended sonorities are those that appear as Bm7/E or Am7/D. These are minor seventh chords with a different bass note. The resulting sonority is an even further extended chord.

The flavor of the melody is changed through the use of extended chords. Some may not find the sound to their liking; perhaps a different reharmonization would be more acceptable. Others will find the new sound that is produced with the harmonization of the last verse interesting and fresh. Using the lyric sheet below, follow along with the taped example; chords are placed above the words on which they occur.

 Traditional, arr. Key, "The Water Is Wide"

```
         G          C  G        D Em  G    D
The water is wide, I can't cross over, and neither have I wings to fly


         G                       C      D   C       G
Oh go and get me a little boat, and we both shall row, my true love and I.




         Cmaj7    Cmaj9    Am7  Bm Bm/A    Em7/G Dadd9
Oh love is warm when it       is  new, and     love    is

Cmaj9          Bm7/E  D7   Am7/G
sweet     when it     is   true.



Am7     Bm7/E     D7  Gmaj7   Am7    G/B Am7/C  Em7/D
But     love    grows old,    and    wax - es   cold,
```

Bm7	Cadd9	Am7/D	Cmaj9	Bm7	Am7	D7sus	D7 G
and	fades	a -	way	like	morn-ing		dew.

WRITTEN ASSIGNMENT

A. Spell the following chords in the given major keys.

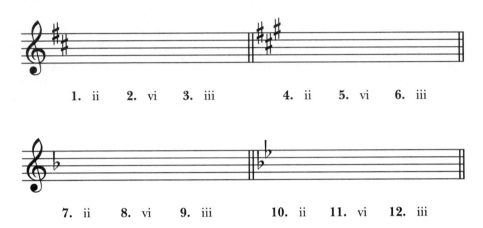

1. ii   2. vi   3. iii   4. ii   5. vi   6. iii

7. ii   8. vi   9. iii   10. ii   11. vi   12. iii

B. In the space below, add a seventh to each of the chords of section A. Use the proper key signatures. The first is done for you.

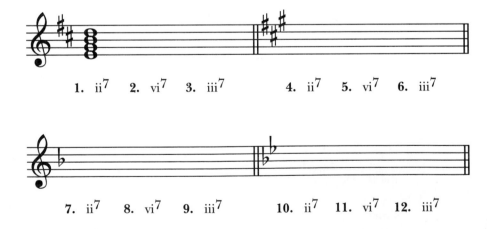

1. ii⁷   2. vi⁷   3. iii⁷   4. ii⁷   5. vi⁷   6. iii⁷

7. ii⁷   8. vi⁷   9. iii⁷   10. ii⁷   11. vi⁷   12. iii⁷

C. Create major seventh chords on the I chords and IV chords in the given major keys.

1. Imaj^7 **2.** IVmaj^7 **3.** Imaj^7 **4.** IVmaj^7

D. In the space below, provide "jazz/pop" chord symbols for each of the examples in sections A, B, and C of the Written Assignment.

A. 1.   2.   3.   4.   5.   6.

  7.   8.   9.   10.   11.   12.

B. 1.   2.   3.   4.   5.   6.

  7.   8.   9.   10.   11.   12.

C. 1.   2.   3.   4.

E. Notate a I–vi–ii–V–I progression in the given major key, spelling chords in root position.

I   vi   ii   V$^{(7)}$ I

F. Notate the same progression, providing a smooth harmonization in the treble staff.

I   vi   ii   V$^{(7)}$ I

CREATIVE ASSIGNMENT

Choose one of the following two options for this assignment:

A. Using a I–vi–ii–V–I progression as a basic motive, create an original melody that will work in conjunction with this harmonic progression. Your composition may be in a major key and meter of your choice. The total length of the composition is also left up to you, as is the instrumentation. Save your composition on the Creative-Assignment tape, and notate your creation.

B. Create an original folklike melody in the major key and meter of your choice. Harmonize your melody two different ways, first using basic triads, then with extended chords. Use major, minor, and dominant 7 chords. Save your composition on the Creative-Assignment tape, and provide written notation, using jazz/pop chord symbols.

JOURNAL ENTRY SUGGESTION

Sometimes performers try to add spice to a piece by using some of the extended chords discussed in this chapter. As pointed out, though, not every piece of music lends itself to such treatment. Can you think of particular pieces that you feel require just the "bare bones" of harmonic treatment?

♪♪♪♪♪♪

Modes and the Minor Scale

Our discussions of melody and harmony have been limited to examples in major keys, with *do* as a tonal center, and melodic and harmonic patterns that support the tendency to pull away from and come back to this focal point. Music is not limited to these patterns, however. We can use the notes of a major scale but choose another tonal center. If we are careful with the melodic patterns we create and with our treatment of harmony, another note can serve as the tonic, giving the music a completely different sound and feeling.

MODES

If we use the notes of a major scale but start on a pitch other than *do*, we are using a *mode*. We could use the C major scale beginning on its second note and continue up to the next octave. *Re* would be our new tonal center.

Ex. 24.1

C major scale   Mode beginning on *re*

Just as the specific arrangement of pitches with *do* as its tonal center is called a major scale, different modes have their own names. The mode that uses the notes of the major scale beginning on *re* is called the *dorian mode*. This mode is common in some Western church music and folk music. "The Meeting at Peterloo," an English ballad, uses the dorian mode. The version notated below begins on *re* of the F major scale; it uses the *G dorian mode*. G tells us which note serves as the tonal center; *dorian* informs us that the G is the second note of the F major scale.

Ex. 24.2

The melody begins with a D pickup, or anacrusis. Longer note values (dotted half notes) identify cadence points. The first and final cadences are on the tonal center of G. Internal cadences use D and F as resting points. In the G dorian mode, D and F serve as the *dominant* pitches, just as *sol* did in the major keys. A cadence on one of these nontonic notes serves to heighten tension and delay the sense of resolution, until we come home to the tonic.

This melody could be written in other dorian modes. If we wanted the piece to be in D dorian, we would use a C major key signature—D dorian implies the second note of the C major scale.

Ex. 24.3

We can start on other notes of the major scale to create music in other modes. Another common mode is the *mixolydian mode,* which begins on the fifth note of the major scale. This note serves as the tonal center in the mixolydian mode. Example 16.1 on page 134 has G as a tonal center but uses the key signature of C major. The melody uses the fifth note of the C major scale as tonic; it uses the *G mixolydian mode.*

Ex. 24.4

The dorian and mixolydian modes are common in Western folk music and sacred music. The rich sound of music in these modes is one explanation for the historical development of music that uses these tonal centers. A Celtic harpist or flutist, limited to the diatonic notes of one major scale, would expand the melodic and harmonic vocabulary of his or her compositions by choosing another note of the scale to use as a tonal center. The arrangement of major and minor seconds within the melodic patterns would be changed, and the harmonies used to accompany melodies would be new and exciting. The modes were first used in Western church music as well as in folk music of various countries. The use of the major scale as the predominant melodic "alphabet" is a relatively recent phenomenon in the history of music.

Another mode, the *aeolian mode,* uses as its tonal center the sixth note of the major scale. This mode has survived (and prospered) as our *minor scale.* In Western art music, this mode has come to be the most common alternative to the major mode. The Chapter 6 listening example "Dies Irae" is an example of a melody that uses the aeolian mode. The notes of the C major scale are utilized, but the sixth note of the scale, A, is the tonal center. Example 24.5 is a notated version of this melody.

Ex. 24.5

It is interesting to note that this melody, part of the Requiem Mass, uses the aeolian mode. We learned in Chapter 2 that the early Greeks associated certain sounds with certain emotions and reactions. For some time, the aeolian mode has been used to portray great sadness—it is the mode of choice for laments and dirges. We cannot be sure if this association evolved over time or has its basis in the inherent quality of the relationship of the pitches themselves. In either case, the associative response to music in the aeolian mode is often a strong one.

THE MINOR SCALE

The aeolian mode survives as a common source of melodic and harmonic material. It is used so extensively that it has come to be recognized as another "scale," the minor scale.

In its original form, the minor scale is known more specifically as the *natural minor scale*. The arrangement of major and minor 2nds found in the natural minor scale is shown here:

Ex. 24.6

This scale, the aeolian mode, shares the notes of a major scale; it is related to the major scale. In this case, the A minor scale, using the notes of the C major scale, is said to be the *relative minor* of C major. The E minor scale, starting on the sixth note of the G major scale, is the relative minor of the G major scale.

Ex. 24.7

With each of these natural minor scales, we can see that the arrangement of major 2nds and minor 2nds is different from the arrangement found in a major scale. In a natural minor scale, minor 2nds are found between the second and third pitches of the scale, and between the fifth and sixth notes. This gives the scale a different sound from the major scale. We can hear this difference in sound if we compare music that is in a minor key to music that has a major tonality. Refer to your listening tape to review the sound of the following examples. Try to determine which examples are major and which are minor.

Key, Trio for Recorders (from Chapter 1)

Traditional, arr. Winston, "Carol of the Bells" (from Chapter 1)

Traditional, arr. Winston, "The Holly and the Ivy" (from Chapter 2)

Bach, Fugue (from Chapter 4)

The first two examples are in a minor key, while the second two are in a major key. The style of the recorder trio is similar to that of the Johann Sebastian Bach fugue, but the tonality is different. The trio uses melodic patterns in D minor, while the fugue is in E♭ major. The quality of the sound is different between major and minor tonalities.

The George Winston arrangements are both of Christmas carols. "Carol of the Bells" is in a minor key, while "The Holly and the Ivy" uses patterns in a major key.

The Melodic Minor Scale

The minor scale is seldom used in its natural form. Often, either the melodic minor or harmonic minor versions are used. The *melodic minor scale* begins the same as the natural minor but some pitches are altered in its ascending form:

Ex. 24.8

We can see and hear this arrangement at work in melodies that have an ascending contour. To provide a stronger sense of movement to the higher tonic, the sixth and seventh scale degrees are raised. This pulls us home when the melody is moving toward the higher tonal center. This change is not needed as the scale descends, so the melodic minor scale is often indicated in its entirety as seen in Example 24.9.

Ex. 24.9

The climb to the upper tonic is enhanced by raising the pitches just before the tonal center. Descending, we move away from this high point, and lower the pitches as we move to the lower tonic.

The Harmonic Minor Scale

While providing a unique and interesting set of possibilities for melodic development, the natural minor scale has some problems when we try to use it as source material for harmonization. I, IV, and V chords in a major key become *minor* chords in a minor key:

Ex. 24.10
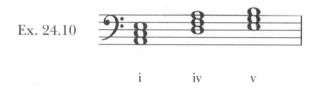

      i   iv   v

The resulting i, iv, and v chords reinforce the minor tonality, but there is something missing when we use these chords in a harmonic progression. In a major key, the I, IV, and V chords do more than strengthen the major tonality; they provide direction to the harmonic progression. This is especially true of the V chord. The seventh scale degree, *ti*, found as the third of the V chord, pulls to the tonic of the I chord. With the minor v chord in a minor key, this half-step polarity is missing. To restore this minor 2nd movement, the v chord is artificially made *major* by raising the seventh note of the scale to create a *harmonic minor scale:*

Ex. 24.11

Some might consider this to be a less *melodic* pattern of notes. Music of the Western world does not often use this specific arrangement of pitches for a melody—the melodic minor version would be used instead. Other cultures, of course, find this scale (or ones similar to it) to be very workable. In Western art music, the harmonic minor scale serves the purpose of providing the minor mode with a much-needed *major* V chord:

Ex. 24.12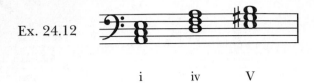

i   iv   V

We can now create a i–iv–V–i progression that reinforces minor tonality with minor i and iv chords *and* supports motion to the tonic with a *major* V chord. The major V, with *ti* as the third of the chord, helps pull to the tonic of the i chord.

Ex. 24.13

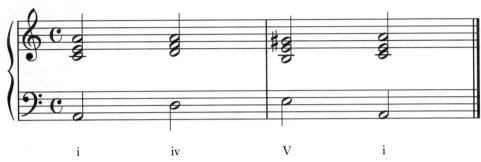

i   iv   V   i

With the harmonic minor version of the scale, as with the melodic minor version, we no longer have the sound of a pure mode. We have adjusted the original arrangement of pitches, taking advantage of what we know about melodic and harmonic tendencies to create and resolve tension in new and interesting ways.

WRITTEN ASSIGNMENT

A. Spell the following modes, using the clef of your choice and applying the appropriate key signature for each.

1. D dorian   **2.** A mixolydian

3. E dorian   **4.** B dorian

5. F mixolydian   **6.** B aeolian

7. A dorian   **8.** D mixolydian

9. G aeolian   **10.** C dorian

B. Identify the mode employed for each of the examples below, then practice singing each, using singing syllables or a neutral syllable.

Traditional Irish, "The Parting Glass"

Traditional Scottish, "The Gobbie-O"

Fifteenth-century English carol, "Agincourt Carol"

Traditional Irish air, "She Moved Through the Fair"

CREATIVE ASSIGNMENT

Try your hand at composing an original modal melody. Be sure to carefully prepare and support the tonal center, avoiding the *do* and *sol* of the major key and using the tonic and dominant tendencies in the mode you have chosen. Work with a meter of your choice and make your melody a length that suits the composition. Save your composition on your Creative-Assignment tape, and notate the melody.

JOURNAL ENTRY SUGGESTION

The use of modes is not limited to folk and church music. Some popular music makes use of modes, and rock music often uses these other forms of tonal arrangements. Can you identify modes at work in any of the music you listen to? Does there seem to be a difference in your response to different modes, or do they seem the same to you?

Glossary

accent mark a wedge-shaped symbol used above or below a notehead to indicate that the pitch is to be emphasized.

accidental any of the symbols used to raise or lower a pitch or to cancel a previous sign or a key signature.

adagio tempo marking for music that is very slow.

agogic accent indicates that a pitch or series of pitches should be given extra weight.

aleatoric music compositions that leave one or more elements of the performance in the hands of the performer.

allegro tempo marking for music that is fast.

amplitude volume.

anacrusis pickup note or notes.

andante tempo marking for music that is slow (walking pace).

antecedent phrase the first phrase of a two-phrase period.

arpeggio a broken chord; perform-ing the pitches of a chord melodically, one after the other.

binary form a song form of two sections.

bodhran a hand-held frame drum used in Celtic music.

cadence a resting point in music.

chironomic notation an early form of music notation that indicates the general contour and accents of the music.

chord three or more pitches sounding at the same time.

chromatic scale an organized series of pitches moving in half steps.

complex meter a meter that combines groupings of twos and threes.

compound meter a meter in which the pulse divides into threes.

conjunct motion stepwise melodic motion.

consequent phrase the second (answering) phrase of a two-phrase period.

contrasting period a period in

217

which the second phrase is different from the first.

cut time   a $\frac{2}{2}$ meter.

diabolus in musica   *see* tritone.

diatonic   music that stays in one key.

disjunct motion   melodic motion that uses leaps of intervals.

dominant chord   the chord built on the fifth note of the scale.

dynamics signs   (such as *p* or *mf*) used to indicate different levels of intensity in music.

enharmonic   term used to describe different names given to the same pitch (G♯ and A♭ are *enharmonic*).

exact repetition   repetition of melodic material that uses the same pitches and rhythm.

final cadence   harmonic cadence that finishes on the tonic chord.

flat sign   notational symbol used to lower a pitch a half step.

form   structure.

fugue   a strict form of imitation.

grand staff   a combined treble staff and bass staff.

half cadence   harmonic cadence point on the V chord.

half step   the smallest intervallic distance used in Western music.

homophonic texture   melody with chords.

intensity   level of loudness in music.

interval   the distance between pitches.

interval of the devil   *see* tritone.

key signature   the arrangement of sharps or flats found at the beginning of each line of music to indicate the tonal center of the music.

ledger line   a small line placed above or below the staff used to temporarily extend the staff.

melodic contour   the shape a melody takes.

melody   a coherent series of pitches.

messa di voce   gradually getting louder, then softer on a sustained pitch.

meter   the organization of rhythmic pulses into groupings of twos, threes, or a combination thereof.

moderato   tempo marking for music that moves at a moderate speed.

monophonic texture   music that has only one melody, without other parts or chords.

motive   a short rhythmic or melodic idea.

natural sign   symbol used to cancel a previously used sharp or flat.

notation   the procedure for writing music on paper.

ostinato   a short musical idea that repeats consistently.

parallel period   a grouping of two phrases in which the second phrase begins exactly like the first.

period   a grouping of two or more phrases.

phrase   a unit of musical syntax, usually forming part of a larger unit.

pitch   how high or low a sound is.

polyphonic texture   texture created when two or more melodies are layered together at the same time.

presto   tempo marking for music that is very fast.

requiem   mass for the dead.

rhythm   the pattern of movement in time.

rondo   a musical form that alternates

an A section with contrasting material.

sequential repetition   melodic repetition that involves the same rhythm with the same series of pitches starting at a higher or lower step.

sharp   symbol used to raise a pitch a half step.

song form   a basic musical structure of either two contrasting sections (labeled AB) or three sections (ABA).

staff   the five lines and the spaces between them that serve as the graph for music notation.

subdominant chord   chord built on the fourth note of the scale.

tempo   the speed of the movement of pulses.

ternary form   a song form of three parts.

texture   the general pattern of sound created when the horizontal and vertical aspects of music are combined.

theme and variations   a musical form that presents a theme, then a series of varied versions of that theme.

timbre   tone color.

tonal center   the pitch that serves as a home note in a melody or harmonic progression.

tone painting   portraying the text of a piece of music through musical means.

triad   a three-note chord.

tritone   the interval of a diminished fifth (or augmented fourth).

Index

A

Absolute music, 11, 31
Accent, 152–53, 158, 199, 217
Accidental, 100, 103, 107, 109, 112, 162, 189, 195, 217
Affections, doctrine of, 11, 81
Agogic accent, 153, 217
Air column instruments, 26
Aleatoric, 67, 217
Anacrusis, 143, 145, 207, 217
Arch. *See* Melodic contour
Ascending contour. *See* Melodic contour
Association, 1, 12, 23, 33, 209
Associative response, 11–14, 22–23, 32, 46, 49, 52, 209. *See also* Response
Attack, 5–6, 24–25, 29, 153

B

Bagpipes, 12
Barline, 116, 131
Bassoon, 5, 26
Blues; blues progression, 160, 189–90, 193, 196, 198
Bodhran, 38, 217
Brass instruments, 27, 31, 49

C

Cadence, 41, 44, 46, 95, 121, 151, 184, 192, 197, 217. *See also* Half cadence; Full cadence; Final cadence; Harmonic cadence

Cadence point, 6, 15, 19, 20, 87, 121, 123, 136, 138, 146, 199, 207
Chance music. *See* Aleatoric
Chant, 48–49, 57
Chromatic scale, 102, 217
Climax point, 6, 10, 12, 15, 19, 20, 29, 41–43, 145
Contrasting period. *See* Period
Conjunct motion, 43, 50, 71, 81, 85, 137–38, 153, 171, 178, 187, 197, 215
Cut time, 127, 129, 218

D

Decay, 5–6, 24
Definite pitch. *See* Pitch
Descending contour. *See* Melodic contour
Diabolus in musica. See Tritone
Diatonic, 162, 208, 218
Dies Irae, 48–49, 61, 208
Disjunct motion, 43, 71, 81, 85, 178, 218
Double bar, 116, 131
Double reed instruments, 26
Dynamics, 63, 111, 153, 158, 218

E

Emotional response, 2, 11–14, 33, 81, 132. *See also* Response
Enharmonic, 102, 218
Envelope of sound, 5, 8, 24
Exact repetition, 58, 138, 218